FROM FOLLY
TO FOLLIES

MICHEL SAUDAN
SYLVIA SAUDAN-SKIRA

FROM FOLLY TO FOLLIES

DISCOVERING THE WORLD OF GARDENS

EVERGREEN

EVERGREEN is an imprint of Benedikt Taschen Verlag GmbH

© for this edition: 1997 Benedikt Taschen Verlag GmbH
Hohenzollernring 53, D–50672 Köln
© 1987 ATELIER D´ÉDITION «LE SEPTIÈME FOU», Geneva
Text, illustrations, layout and conception: Michel Saudan and Sylvia Saudan-Skira, Geneva
Introduction: François Crouzet
Cover: Mark Thomson, London

Printed in Italy
ISBN 3-8228-8275-5
GB

CONTENTS

INTRODUCTION

*A*ll gardens are built by children. Unfortunately, children eventually grow up and become adults. They learn that everything they thought was unique is in fact banal, and everything they thought eternal is transitory. They discover that all that they loved is frail and mortal.

Later on, and more pleasantly, they will make another discovery: Although all life eventually ends, it continually renews itself. More beautiful than the garden itself are the memories of it—the regrets, the dreams, and the ghosts of gardens that we see in our mind's eye when we sniff a bunch of flowers or close our eyes and think of gardens of the past.

On his way to America, French author and statesman Chateaubriand called on the governor of Saint-Pierre, the French territory in the Atlantic:

A fine, soft aroma of heliotrope was being given off by a little bed of flowering beanstalks; it was wafted to our nostrils not by a breeze from our homeland, but by a wild wind from the New World, which bore no relationship to the exiled plant and none of the voluptuous memories it normally aroused. This perfume had not been breathed by beauty, or purified in her breast, or left in the air as she passed by. But the scent was charged with memories of daybreak, of human culture and the world outside; it had in it all the melancholy of regret, partings, and lost youth.

And Proust, near the beginning of *A la recherche du temps perdu*:

When this humble passerby contemplated it, this dreaming child fixed this little corner of nature in his mind, the garden could not have realized that because of him all its most fleeting, ephemeral details would live on and not be forgotten. And yet the hawthorn perfume that gathers honey along the hedge where the wild roses will soon take its place, the sound of muffled, unechoing footsteps on a gravel path, a bubble forming against a water plant by the water in the river and bursting straight away: all these details, because they gave me such exaltation when I saw them, have survived despite the passing of time, even though the paths themselves are no more and the people who once crowded them are long since dead.

These two passages are disturbingly alike, like a voice and its echo, or an object and its reflection in the water.

Gardens are memories. Their history is rooted in ancient Greece and Rome, influenced to a greater or lesser extent by the Egyptians, the Persians, the Turks, and the Chinese. In Europe, the history of the garden begins and ends with the Italians. But the French in many ways played the most important part in this history. Although the idea of the garden as a gradual progress toward initiation developed in Renaissance Italy, with the final epiphany in the depths of a woods, and the English who dreamed up the studied unkemptness of the "Anglo-Chinese" garden, the French achievement lay in the refusal ever to lose sight of the fact that man is a part of nature.

The next word belongs to Charles Perrault, the great French writer of fairy tales—and what is a garden if not a fairy tale?—who told an anecdote that encapsulates the French attitude to the garden as a place for the delectation of man:

When the Tuileries had been replanted and brought to the state in which you see them now, Monsieur Colbert [Louis XIV's Chief Minister] said to me, "Let us go to the Tuileries." He condemned the open gates of the garden: "This garden should be kept for the king alone. The people should not be allowed to ruin it, for give them a little time and they will destroy it totally." His opinion seemed to me to be very hard on the people of Paris. As we walked along the broad avenue, I said to him, "Sir, you would not believe the respect everyone has for these gardens, right down to the humblest of artisans. The women and children not only studiously avoid picking flowers, but will not even touch them. They walk through the gardens like reasonable people; the gardeners will bear witness to this fact. It would be a major affliction for the public not to be able to come and walk in these gardens."

"The only people who come here are idle good-for-nothings," he said to me. "People come here," I replied, "to recover from their illnesses and take the air. They come here to talk of business, marriage, and anything that is better talked about in a garden than in a church, which is where they would have to meet if there were no gardens. I am convinced," I continued, "that the gardens of kings are so grand and spacious that all their children can walk there as well."

He smiled as I said this, and since as we spoke most of the gardeners had assembled before him, he asked them whether the people did not cause a great deal of harm to the gardens. "Not at all, Monseigneur," they replied, almost with one voice. "They are perfectly happy to walk up and down and look without touching."

Monsieur Colbert walked around the gardens, gave his orders, and never spoke again of barring the gates to anyone who wanted to come in.

This scene could almost have been written by Molière. It is the timeless dialogue of the deaf between the voice of reason and the calculating and arrogant technocrat who is convinced that right is on his side but miraculously changes his mind and joins the side of reason, pretending that he has been on that particular side all along. Most important, it shows that here is a garden for the French men and women of the seventeenth century: a *salon*, a place for meeting and discussion, surrounded by the beauties of nature. A century later they were doing things the other way around, bringing nature into their *salons*. Herein, perhaps, lies the main difference between the English garden and the French one.

Parisians go to the Tuileries or the Jardin des Plantes for the same reason the man or woman in Madrid goes to church, or someone living in Naples, Rome, or Siena goes to the main city square. They go for pleasure and for more serious matters: love, health, family discussions, getting on with their everyday existence. They are not Neoplatonists or eccentric country gentlemen or young people with high ideals like Goethe's Werther: They are ordinary, reasonable people.

So the garden reflects life, a model and symbol of the reason that governs our lives, the art of making our way through life, and is also a source of diversions, dreams, and follies. The clear, fresh water of a water basin or fountain reflects the clarity of the poet's soul. "Everything that is strange about man, all that is flighty and unpredictable, is contained in a simple two-syllable word: 'garden.' " So says Louis Aragon.

So is a garden a symbol of wisdom, or of folly?

Although at first sight a garden seems no more than a pleasant work of fantasy through which we can wander as our whims take us, it soon becomes apparent that there is a clearly defined intention at work behind the scenes. The garden is a path we are all meant to follow, even though the route may not necessarily be the most pleasant or convenient. But as Kierkegaard said, "It is not the road that is difficult, but the difficulty that is the road." So everything in the garden gradually takes shape, and gradually we can decipher the intention behind its creation, a subtle system of existence and a general philosophy of nature. And slowly and gradually the meaning of the garden rises to the surface like a shipwreck emerging from the depths of the ocean.

Gardens are a part of the European artistic heritage: A garden by Lancelot "Capability" Brown or André Le Nôtre, Versailles or the Boboli Gardens, all bear the marks of the same genius, the same richness of texture, as a Vivaldi concerto, a suite by Bach, or a sculpture by Rodin.

Like the sounds and words of the composer and playwright, the artist's canvas and the sculptor's stone, gardens add to the beauty of the world. They turn enemies into friends. They transmute into beauty our fear of the yawning precipice, the dizziness of the mountainside, and our fear of the dark cavern or the roaring of the waterfall. The garden is a whole world in miniature; it is nature made tangible. It is up to each of us to discover the secret laws that govern it, the "rhétorique profonde" described by Baudelaire.

It is poets, first and foremost, who are served by gardens. For a poet, a garden represents a way of breaking down the walls of reason and reuniting man's heart with the essence of existence, which he lost when he ceased to be an innocent child. It reminds him of the enchantment of love, the fleetingness of time, the bitter blows of disappointment, the marvelous and yet despairing redolence of memory, the ceaseless round of lost happiness, shadows, and death.

For Ronsard, Hölderlin, Musset, Heine, Nerval, Verlaine, and Rilke, the garden imparts a delicate, intangible perfume. The garden had a unique fascination for them, for they held the key to the mysteries of the grotto and the enchantment of the fountain, where Narcissus saw himself reflected and was drowned. Sighs the echo of Valéry's Narcissus:

Remember me and dream, fair fountains, for without
Your dreams, my beauty and my pain would be in doubt.

Fountains reflect the music of words. Since gardens have the power to transport us through time and space, from Italy to England and from Germany to France, from the Renaissance to the nineteenth century, from intricate flower beds to vast, sweeping panoramas, they have struck a particular chord with painters and musicians, playwrights and, especially, poets. We never have to look very far for references to the garden. Throughout history people have yearned to return to the Garden of Eden. As Francis Bacon said, "God Almighty first planted a garden. And indeed it is the purest of human pleasures." And Baudelaire's great lost garden was a repository of memories, sights, sounds, and odors:

> The verdant paradise, the childhood love that thrills:
> We ran, and sang, and kissed, and gave each other flowers;
> The violins resonated through the hills,
> As we drank wine within the wooded bower.

But gardens do not function only sensually or aesthetically. Look at Robinson Crusoe. Once he has set up home on his desert island, complete with palisades and ramparts to deter the foe, and has stockpiled life's necessities—weapons, tools, furniture, provisions—he still has one vital need: In the middle of his island he builds himself a little garden complete with trellises and shaded retreats.

So it seems as though all of us have an innate need for the refreshment and spiritual succor provided by the garden. At least, those of us who belong to "civilized" society. The savage has no need for a garden, nor can he understand why we do. He is already a part of nature; to him, the garden is unnatural and unnecessary. It is a piece of fiction that city dwellers have agreed to believe in.

The art of creating a garden is not far from the art of writing poetry. This is not simply because the choice and arrangement of words are akin to the choice of scents, the shaping of trees and hedges and the layout of paths between them. The garden both reshapes and transmutes nature, making it more than the sum of its parts. In the same way, poetry metamorphoses individual words. Art becomes an ethic, and ethic becomes art. No one has expressed this better than Nietzsche, who said: "Any ethic is contrary to freedom: it is tyranny over Nature and Reason." The main distinguishing feature of any system of ethics, and that which gives it its incalculable value, is that it is a long-term constraint of nature. If we are to understand a philosophy like Stoicism or Puritanism, we can only do so by realizing that language acquires vitality and freedom by the act of being constrained: Meter, rhythm, and rhyme liberate language by constraining it. Those of a utilitarian frame of mind see this as folly and extravagance, and the anarchists and freethinkers of this world regard it as submission to a set of arbitrary laws. But strange though it may seem, nothing that has broken new ground in the history of human thought, politics, art, or ethics has ever been able to flourish without the tyranny of such arbitrary laws.

It was no mere coincidence that the art of the garden reached what was probably its greatest level of perfection, with the ensuing decadence, at the same time that European civilization reached its apogee and began a long decline. The gardens of the late eighteenth century reflected a happiness that was nearing its end. The guillotine was at hand, and its arrival heralded that of the chainsaw. Eventually people stopped creating gardens in preference to wide open spaces with lawns, paths, woods, and ornamental buildings. From being objects of aesthetic admiration, gardens had turned to places of recreation.

At the time of the Prince de Ligne, in the eighteenth century, gardens were the symbol of the level of perfection European civilization had reached, and people were very clear about what they wanted from their gardens. Knowing that their gardens were there to be enjoyed gave them almost as much pleasure as the act of enjoying them. "Apart from my children, and the two or three women I love, or think I love, to distraction," wrote the Prince de Ligne, "my gardens give me more pleasure than anything else in the world; there are few so beautiful as they. One of my greatest pleasures lies in making them even finer to behold; and yet I am almost never there."

There was a great deal of foresight in gardens of this time, for they were full of symbols of death: tombs, broken columns, cenotaphs, and funerary urns. Ornamental buildings were often deliberately built in ruins; although they were follies, there was a sad note of wisdom in them too. As well as foreshadowing death, they were a reminder that there were enemies lying in wait: people like Sade, Rousseau, Beethoven, and Hugo. Sade shuns open space; his landscapes are full of walls, forests, and precipices. Rousseau's maniacal false naiveté lies in turning gardens into jungles. There is no excusing the destruction wrought by Rousseau by saying it is unintentional. "You should have shown remorse before the crime, not after it," as the judge says to the man in the dock. Beethoven is a man of tempests and heroics, the genius who freed art from the use of carefully defined shape and form. Without form there can be no gardens. His *Pastoral* Symphony dealt a heavy blow to the garden-owning aristocracy and heralded the era of village democracy. And Victor Hugo saw any attempt to organize nature as a threat. Anything that prevented it from flourishing and spreading weakened it as well:

> The dreamer fears the gate and iron stakes.
> Freedom, among the ploughshares and the rakes,
> Sings loudest in green pastures and blue sky.
> 'Tis Man builds gardens; fields doth God supply.

But in an age where there are no more gates and railings, gardens lose their *raison d'être*. Every garden owner created his garden in his own image and took pleasure in giving pleasure to others. Now, in an age where land is common property, people are no longer so enchanted by the garden. The utopias that were supposed to liberate the soul have attained perfection in cement and concrete.

Gardens are not meant to free the soul or reveal a hidden truth. They are created to dazzle the eye and enchant the heart. They are pure pageantry and splendor. Gardens are poetry, not truth. It must surely have been in a garden, perhaps his own at Beloeil, that the Prince de Ligne wrote this Mozartian effusion to a lady friend, the swansong of a dying European civilization:

> I do not see the woman whom I love with all my heart, but I received a letter from her yesterday and I shall receive another from her tomorrow. In a few days I will go to see her whom I love so much, for she is not far away. Now I am at my chores: I have paper and ink in front of me, and I am alone; that is the present. When she left me, she said she loved me; that is the past. When I see her again, she will tell me she loves me; that is the future. Until then I am happy and I sing for joy when I awake in the morning.

Such is the power of the garden.

O N E

THE PATH TO INITIATION

*Italy in the
Sixteenth
and Seventeenth
Centuries*

Frascati, Rome
Gardens of the Villa Aldobrandini, 1601–21
Giacomo Della Porta, Carlo Maderno, and
Giovanni Fontana
Grotto and spring of initiation

The Renaissance was an age of impatience. Man began to feel a tension underlying his existence and there began a debate about man and his power that has never been absent from Western consciousness to this day.''[1] Eventually this debate was to overturn the centuries-old relationship between man and nature, for man was beginning to realize the power he had over his environment. No longer was he subject to a symbolic power inherent in nature, a source of good in his life but at the same time unpredictable, controlling his destiny. The relationship between man and nature was now a battle of wills, between man and his powers of reason on one hand and the mysteries of nature on the other. His scientific knowledge now enabled him to provide positive, rational answers to questions about the nature of reality. Man's role in the universe moved from being a passive one to an active one.

In order to change his relationship with the world around him, Renaissance man had to learn how to define its physical boundaries and bring up to date those theories that allowed him to make sense of reality. There were already two fundamental laws governing reality: *finitio*, defining every object in mathematical terms, and *collocatio*, locating objects in relation to their environment. The theorist Leon Battista Alberti added a third, *concinnitas*, or the law of harmony: "Harmony is the name I give to that which accompanies the soul and reason, and which manifests itself in vast areas of creation. It embraces the whole of man's life and his laws, and covers the whole of nature."[2] Since life was governed by this law relating one part of the whole to another, "so that there is a mutual concord between their outward appearances,"[3] ineluctable relationships now existed between a piece of architecture and its surrounding space. No longer was the meaning of a building defined by the walls that enclosed it; there had to be an organized relationship between the interior and the exterior.

Alberti came from a family of Florentine merchants but was living in exile. When Alberti returned to Florence in 1439, the city had been under the protective wing of the powerful and influential Medici family. Its illustrious representative at the time, Cosimo the Elder, had surrounded himself with a circle of artists and scholars, his Academy of Plato, ever since he became the family's figurehead. An active patron of the arts and a great pragmatist, he immediately made it his task to make full use of his architectural heritage. Influenced by the humanists in whose company he spent so much time, he was greatly attracted by the idea of a new type of building for the new age he lived in, first described and built by the ancients: the villa. But for Cosimo and the Medicis, the villa would serve first and foremost as a reflection of the image they wanted themselves to have. The villa was an "open" building, sensitive to the surrounding space, not defensive like the castles that had come before, and it was a perfect mirror both of the Medicis' initiative and their great skill in the art of trade and finance. At the same time it was a symbol of their prestige in a way that a palace hidden away in the dark, narrow streets of the city could not be.

Within thirty years, Michelozzo, the court architect, had transformed Cosimo's feudal castles—Trebbio, near Cafaggiolo (1427–36), Cafaggiolo itself (1451), and Careggi (1457)—into magnificent villas and then built a new villa at Fiesole (1458–61). At Cafaggiolo, Careggi, and Fiesole, the grounds were still constructed in traditional style, a series of enclosed spaces separated by walls or hedges like the *hortus conclusus* of the monasteries, not directly related to the interior of the villa.

While Michelozzo was building the villa at Fiesole for Cosimo, in 1459 Alberti was commissioned by the Rucellai family to build the Villa Quaracchi. This was the opportunity Alberti had been seeking, to create a harmonic relationship between the villa and its surrounding gardens. We see this clearly is his writings, in particular in the theories he sets out in his *De re aedificatoria*, where he relates the practical craft of architecture to his theories about the harmony of the universe. With studious attention to the architecture of antiquity, he created elements that joined one space to another: loggias, porticoes, galleries—all essential elements if the building as a whole was to be in harmony with the outside world. He argued also that these parts of a building should be decorated with *trompe l'oeil* outdoor scenes, to create an imaginary as well as a real relationship between architecture and its natural environment. Above all, he urged architects to find a new set of rules for treating the space outside the building, which should be based on the study of the architecture of antiquity.

Eight years after Alberti died, Cosimo's grandson, Lorenzo de'Medici, summoned Giuliano da San Gallo to his court and commissioned a sumptuous villa from him. His task was to restore the former castle of Poggio, at Caiano, which the Medicis had bought from the Strozzi family.

San Gallo undertook the project in complete acceptance of Alberti's new vocabulary of classical architecture. His exploration of the buildings of antiquity (shown in the meticulous drawings he made from the buildings themselves) was a constant inspiration and guide. The use of elements such as the portico topped by a tympanum, the terrace opening the villa to the outside, and the interplay of monumental staircases was reminiscent of the Roman villa, but at the same time they allowed the interior of the building to spill out into the exterior in line with Alberti's theories of harmony. The gardens were intended to continue this effect, but when Lorenzo died in 1492, work on the villa was incomplete and it was never finished according to the original plan. The major architectural commissions, which were an expression of the prince's magnificence, also came to a halt. In 1492 Florence entered a troubled period in its history, and order was not restored until much later, in 1537, when Pope Cosimo I came to power. In the meantime the popes and cardinals of Rome took up the role of building villas, which hitherto had been the preserve of the great families of Florence.

Rome once again became the seat of the papacy in 1420 and was gradually emerging from a long period of lethargy. Its magnificent ruins were unable to hide the fact that it resembled an abandoned city gradually being taken over by the infertile and unhealthy marshlands of the surrounding countryside. From the moment he was elected in 1447, Pope Nicholas V began to restore Rome's proud position as the papal city. Eventually, hastened by the decline of Florence, Rome was once again to become a major center of culture, attracting sculptors, painters, and architects from all over Italy.

At the end of the fifteenth century, Innocent VIII was the first pope to have a villa built on the hills of the Vatican. In 1503 the new pontiff, Julius II, consulted an architect about the land between this villa and the pontifical palace, and this meeting sparked a major change in the way people viewed the relationship between a villa and its gardens. It was Donato Bramante who received this commission, the Cortile of the Belvedere shortly after his arrival in Rome. Bramante viewed the project as three-dimensional at a time when architects were still thinking in terms of two-dimensional space. His interpretation of the gardens even went beyond the concepts of harmony established by Alberti. Bramante still used a frontal perspective to ensure the symmetry of the whole, but he designed the villa and its surroundings as a single, inseparable entity.

Bramante designed a succession of terraces for the Cortile, linked together by monumental staircases and creating the perspective of the whole using an arcaded portico leading to the semicircular rotunda. There an open cupola both acts as a focus for, and redistributes the lines of, the force set up by the interplay of terraces. This was a vision inspired by antiquity, but it was no longer modeled on the villa alone (the villa described by Pliny); instead, it was the villa *and* the gardens built by Hadrian at Tivoli. The Cortile was received enthusiastically by the young architect's contemporaries, but unfortunately Bramante's vision was soon clouded by the building of the Vatican Library.

Nevertheless, the stage had been set, and in 1517 Cardinal Julian de'Medici, the future Pope Clement VII, commissioned the first villa to be built outside the walls of Rome from Raphael, Antonio da San Gallo, and Giulio Romano. The site intended for the villa was an exceptional one, and the project was intended to create a perfect synthesis between the Elysian concept of the Roman villa and a spatial creation combining a theater with loggias and terraces to extend the villa into the countryside and create a formal structure as strict as that of the Cortile. But the sacking of Rome by the troops of Charles V in 1527 put an end to work on the villa and it was never completed.

It was not until the 1540s that the infatuation with villas, begun by Julius II, was renewed. It can be seen not only in Rome but also in Florence, Venice, and all the courts of Europe. Once rebellions had been put down and any leanings toward democracy were stifled, city governments from Venice to Rome grew up in the shadow of the immense power of the two great families of Europe, the Valois and the Hapsburgs. It was essential that the respective courts mirror their prestige, and the festivals held to celebrate alliances between them were of major importance. The new concept of what a garden should be offered a perfect backdrop for a society where intrigue was the most powerful weapon. But submitting

nature and all its symbolic powers to pure architectural theory, even if this theory was rooted in classical antiquity, could succeed only if it could be justified in a reassuring and inspiring way.

This problem was solved by the republication in 1546 of a work that had passed almost unnoticed when it first appeared in 1499, the *Hypnerotomachia Poliphilii*, or *Dream of Poliphilus*, by Francesco Colonna. This book allowed the architect to link the senses to the faculty of reason by way of the imagination, and it created the model for a new type of garden, where the role of reason was to discover the hidden meaning behind nature and, in so doing, to achieve harmony with nature. Architectural references took on a whole new value: The architect now had access to new sources of inspiration without falling prey to sterile intellectualism.

After writing the *Dream*, Francesco Colonna, the son of a highly respected Roman family that had connections with the Orsini and Farnese families, had started to restore the temple of Praeneste (now Palestrina) and rebuild the family palace on the same site. The estates of the Colonna family, including Palestrina, had been razed to the ground in 1436 by the pope's troops. Thus Colonna had to become an archaeologist as well when he embarked on his famous work. His profound knowledge of research carried out by his contemporaries, both architects and philosophers, gave him a breadth of vision whose effects were not felt until sometime later, for the end of the fifteenth century was a time of great spiritual discord.

For its part, the Church was barricading itself behind the Inquisition, and Colonna sought a response through gradual initiation—an initiation that inevitably led to the fulfillment of his desires, both physical and spiritual. Colonna was branded a heretic, and after his book had been published he retired, disheartened and ruined, to the Dominican order. He died in a monastery in Venice in 1527.[4]

The *Dream* describes in words and pictures the adventures of Poliphilus in his search for Polia, or Wisdom. In his quest, he sees forests, caves, ruins, mythical animals, magnificent palaces, strange architecture, and beautiful gardens. Poliphilus gradually realizes that if he can decipher the symbols he finds in these ancient stones, the mysteries of nature will be revealed to him. The *Dream*, a vision set in stone, "is ambiguously redolent both of pleasure and necessity; the concept of sublimation has possibly never been so well illustrated as it is here."[5]

In its use of reason to sublimate the natural, or even the supernatural, the book gave gardens a new significance. When the book was republished, gardens became a place of learning where visitors could refresh their minds as well as their senses. This aesthetic conquest of nature created an alliance between inanimate stones and living vegetation; no clear distinction could be made between statues, ruins, and buildings on the one hand and water and the plant world on the other. The new garden meant that a union was now possible between the faculty of reason and the senses. From now on, allegorical figures, fauns, and nymphs would descend from painted ceilings to illuminate and guide the visitor along the desired path through the garden.

The predetermined route included clearly defined halting places marked by a series of terraces, like the great tiers of the Temple of Fortune at Praeneste. And the gardens that grew up around Florence and Lucca (Castello, then later Pratolini and Collodi) or Rome (Tivoli, Bagnaia, Caprarola, and Frascati) began to resemble the idealized background of the *Dream*.

These gardens, which also functioned as a kind of theatrical stage, were a perfect reflection of the age, for

> They have a total freedom in their design, and a flexibility whereby they could be adapted to the whims of notables of the day. Nothing seemed to be immune to this fashion, which was dominated by the use of symbol, classical decoration, and imagery that both described and formed part of the joys of life. . . . It was as though nature were cooperating with man by agreeing to be used in the service of a prince or a noble.[6]

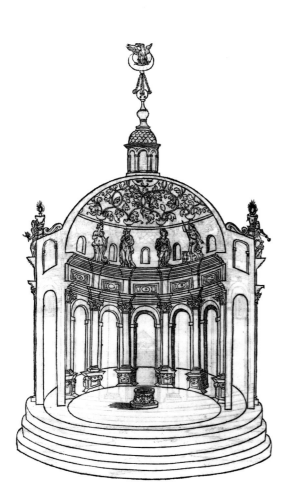

Temple, exterior and section
Francesco Colonna, *Dream of Poliphilus*, 1546

THE PATH THROUGH THE GARDEN: IN THE FOOTSTEPS OF POLIPHILUS

The passion for expansive gardens designed and built by great artists began in the Rome of Julius II, but it rapidly spread to the rest of Italy. The Medicis were no exception. In 1538, a year after he came to power, Cosimo I asked architect and sculptor Niccolò Pericoli, known as "Il Tribolo," to redesign the grounds of his villa in Castello, where he had spent his childhood. The gardens were to reflect those in the *Dream,* for the Medicis had received a copy of the book from the archaeologist Leandro Alberti, the son of the great theorist and a friend of the Colonna family.

Pericoli based his design around a central axis made up of three huge terraces.

The visitor passed through the first, which was mainly open and treeless, into a woods made up of cypress, laurel, and olive trees set so closely together that the sun could barely penetrate. The garden was reminiscent of the *bosco* that Poliphilus enters with such trepidation. This is no longer the case, and for the description of the woods we must rely on Montaigne's account of his visit to Florence.[7] In the middle of the woods was a fountain with a wide basin, pointing out the direction the visitor should follow. This led to an orchard, whose straight lines of potted lemon trees reflected the clarity of the laws governing the world of nature. The orchard was bounded by the wall supporting the last terrace, and in the middle of this the visitor came to a deep, cool grotto. Concealed steps at the side led to the last stopping place on the walk, in the middle of a woods of oak trees, with a powerful allegorical statue by Bartolommeo Ammannati, seemingly embodying all the mystery of nature's life-giving forces.

The gardens at Castello were still unfinished when, in 1549, the duke took on a still larger project. At the behest of his wife, Eleanor of Aragon, who wanted a less austere home for her court than the somewhat somber palace in the Via Larga, Cosimo bought her a sumptuous residence from the Florentine merchant Lucca Pitti. This was located at the gates of Florence, on the left bank of the Arno at a place known as "I Borgoli," or "Bogoli," after a family that owned some meadows there. The name remained attached to the gardens, now known as Boboli, and work began in the same year under the direction of the architect who had built the gardens at Castello.

Here again, Il Tribolo's intention was to base the gardens on the *Dream* and have them slope gently around a central axis, but the beauty of nature would be shown on an even grander scale than before, as a greater area of land was available. But barely a year after he began work, Il Tribolo died suddenly. The work both on Boboli and Castello was entrusted to the young Bartolommeo Ammannati, who, working with Giacomo da Vignola, had just completed a villa in Rome for Pope Julius III. Eleanor asked him also to enlarge the palace by building a huge courtyard overlooking the gardens. By considerably lowering the level of the ground, Ammannati created two separate levels and also a broad horseshoe-shaped amphitheater of greenery. This meant that the upper courtyard now became a great loggia, joined to the gardens by staircases extending down on either side. Thus the route through the gardens appeared suddenly, like a curtain being raised on a stage. This magnificent vista was further enhanced when, in 1608, Giulio and Alfonso Parigi carried out more refinements for Cosimo II.

After 1569, Cosimo gradually relinquished the reins of power and retired from the court. After his wife died, he took up residence at the villa at Castello, his favorite home, where he liked to grow jasmine in the gardens. His son Francesco, who succeeded him in 1574, asked his personal architect, Bernardo Buontalenti, to continue the work on Boboli. He made no changes in the overall design but instead took on the task of building what was essential for the garden to be worthy of the *Dream*—an enchanted grotto.

All the basic elements of the gardens at Boboli were now in place, but the design evolved gradually, from revealing nature to simply displaying it. Eleanor's wishes could be translated into practice only in the exterior, unlike the interior at Castello, where Cosimo constantly sought to rediscover his lost childhood.

At the beginning of the *Dream*, Poliphilus has wandered into a woods where "the trees were so closely packed together and their branches so tightly intertwined"[8] that he is immediately reminded of the terrors of the mythical Minoan labyrinth: "I knew not what I should do, for even if I cried out aloud, it would be in vain, for there was no one to hear me except the fair Echo. . . . I wished I had the pitiable Ariadne there to help me, and the ball of thread that she gave to Theseus to guide him through the labyrinth."[9]

This first labyrinth—Poliphilus later encounters another, which Francesco Colonna traced on the surface of the water—became an essential feature in garden design from the sixteenth century onward. It served to remind visitors of the image of the hero passing through the forest and perpetuated the theme of the long, dark, winding road found in Greek and Roman antiquity, most notably in Crete. The road was strewn with obstacles, which the adventurer had to overcome before reaching the magic grotto, where the truth would be revealed in the moment of initiation.

This close relationship between the labyrinth and the grotto, linked with the idea of the return to life, or rebirth, can be seen in many Italian gardens, including Castello, Boboli, and Caprarola, and the tradition continued into the next century,

Giusto Utens
Halfmoon panels, c. 1599
ABOVE: Pitti Palace and Boboli Gardens, Florence
OPPOSITE: Villa Medici, Castello, Florence

THE MAZE: A TEST OF FORTITUDE

where it can be seen at Verona or Collodi. By this time its function had become a purely decorative one, and it can be found in many different forms. Many designs, particularly those of Charles Estienne and Vredeman de Vries, make abundant use of the Dedalus, as the maze was known, to ornament flower beds because of the elegance created by its strict geometry. Bushes and hedges were cut as low as possible so that the viewer could appreciate the whole design in conjunction with the sweetly scented plants it contained.

WATER LEADS THE VISITOR

When he leaves the labyrinth, Poliphilus finds a spring that leads him onward in his voyage.

Bodies of water were an essential feature of the many gardens that princes and prelates ordered for their new villas. By its very nature, water is a moving, tumbling, musical medium. Poliphilus experienced this himself: "I knelt on the ground at the edge of the fountain, cupped my hands and filled them with this nectar, but as I put it to my mouth, I heard a melodious sound, and the very sweetness of this harmony gave me more pleasure than drinking the water."[10] This idea of the hero under the spell of the water, being led by it to strange new discoveries, was something the designers had very much in mind when they built splendid new gardens in and around Rome for the patriarchs of the Church from 1550 onward. After the sackings of 1527, Tivoli, then Frascati, and even some of the more distant regions, such as the hills around Viterbo, became places of residence for prelates.

The first major project was begun by the Cardinal Bishop of Ferrara, Ippolito d'Este. When he was appointed governor in Tivoli in 1549, he immediately bought all the land in front of the Benedictine monastery, which he was given as a residence. This land, lying to the north, was steep and rocky and covered with forests, but because it was so steep, it had a magnificent view across the Gaudente valley. Work did not begin until ten years after the land was purchased. The cardinal was constantly harassed by Pope Paul IV, who was not impressed by the way some members of the clergy surrounded themselves with such pomp and ceremony.

After the pope died in 1559, the monastery was transformed into a spacious villa, but the main preoccupation of the chief architect, Alberto Galvani of Ferrara, and his workers was the gardens. A large area of Tivoli was dug up so that a 650-yard tunnel could be constructed to divert the river Aniene, which supplied the town with water, and feed the fifty fountains in the garden. Large-scale engineering work had to be carried out to turn the arid land into a series of terraces arranged along two separate axes, modeled partly on the stepped temple at Praeneste, which was so dear to Francesco Colonna. The principal axis, radiating outward from the villa itself, was crossed halfway along its length by transverse axes, which ensured that the gardens did not descend too steeply. Each of these axes—some gently sloping downward, others arranged in steps, some fringed with fountains and little waterfalls—gave a different view at every turn, and water was an essential element. The fountains all have names: the Organ, the Ovato, the Little Rome.

At Tivoli, truth was revealed not in the gradual discovery of the visitor's inner self or through the faculty of reason; rather, the inward harmony of the garden was to be perceived by the senses. Like Poliphilus, visitors must allow themselves to be entranced by the music and light of the water and by its mutability from one minute to the next. The designer of the gardens often used artifice to increase the viewer's involvement. He ordered his *fontanieri* to outdo Mother Nature herself and create musical fountains, where the jets of water made artificial birds sing as they perch on trees with leaves made of leather. The Organ Fountain, for example, used a hydraulic system invented by the Frenchman Claude Venard that was so complex it could play four-part madrigals and motets.

Work continued for twelve years, from 1560 to the death of Ippolito d'Este in 1572. More than twenty artists were involved, but the man who best understood the cardinal's "folly" was Pirro Ligorio, an architect and designer who specialized in the grotesque. A Neapolitan who had lived in Rome from an early age, Ligorio shared his patron's great predilection for antique statuary and was soon caught up in the cardinal's grand vision of a golden age where nymphs, gods, and goddesses rule over the world of nature. Apart from managing his staff, Ligorio personally designed the Avenue of a Hundred Fountains and the Ovato and Girandole fountains. The gardens were a unique creation, an elegant expression of the new awareness of the importance of the space outside a building, where architecture and nature yield to each other. The Villa d'Este was a foretaste of the great designs of the seventeenth century.

The gardens at Tivoli were no more than a building site when those near the small town of Bagnaia, in the province of Latium, were opened in 1568. The Villa Lante had been the residence of the Archbishop of Viterbo since the thirteenth century. In 1566 Francesco Gambara was appointed as the new bishop. He immediately commissioned the architect Jacopo Barozzi, known as "Il Vignola," to transform the hunting lodge at Bagnaia into a grand villa. The cardinal had originally met Barozzi in Rome, where he had been secretary to Pope Julius III and had designed a villa for the pope on the Via Flaminia.

Vignola used a novel idea at Bagnaia. To avoid spoiling the strongly axial shape of the villa and its surroundings, and in fact to emphasize this effect, he designed not one villa but two identical *palazzine*. He preserved the existing pyramidal shape, with a wide terrace at its base, which gradually became narrower as four terraces of decreasing width led away from the first. At the apex, water guides the visitor onward, with the Fountain of Lights, Table of Water, Giants' Fountain, Water Stair, and Fountain of the Deluge. The idea of following the river back to its source, where the initiation takes place, was perfectly expressed. At the end of this route, the visitor reached the most secret part of the garden, where he was met by a grotto with a pavilion, the Chamber of the Muses, at its side. This, and the Fountain of the Deluge, marked the border between two worlds: the world that man has been able to use his knowledge to master and the unknown world, whose mysterious forces he still fears.

The entire route that Vignola designed led toward this point of transition. The strict geometry of the first terrace, heightened at the end of the century by the building of a Moorish fountain (which Vignola had planned but not built), gradually relaxed and gave way to a more flexible, sinuous design that narrowed the gap between man and nature. But nature never took over completely. Even though the artifice we find at Bagnaia is less carefully orchestrated than that at Tivoli, the moment of revelation is still colored by the sensual pleasure of seeing nature subjugated to art.

When Pope Gregory XIII realized how proud his bishop was of the new villa, he saw only the scarcely concealed epicureanism it betrayed and was shocked by the huge expense that had gone into its construction. He immediately suspended payment of the generous pension that was being paid to Gambara. When Gambara died in 1587, the upper part of the garden and its fountains had been completed, but only one of the two *palazzine* had been built and the lower terrace was still bare. The new owner, the cardinal of Montalto, who was the nephew of Sixtus V, took advantage of somewhat more generous support from the pope and was able to commission Carlo Maderno to carry on where Vignola had left off and finish the Moorish fountain. This is a broad, square expanse of water that evokes the naumachia of Roman villas with its little island and four stone boats bearing a trumpet and two arquebusiers spouting water. This was a perfect reflection of Vignola's original conception of the fountain.

Work was almost finished when the cardinal died in 1623, and the villa was given its present name in 1654, when it was presented by Alexander VII to a relative, Ippolito Lante.

When Vignola came to work for Francesco Gambara at Bagnaia, he was not unfamiliar with the area. In 1559 one of the cardinal's friends, Alessandro Farnese, had asked him to put the finishing touches to a huge palace that his uncle, Pope Paul III, had built at Caprarola thirty years before. The palace, designed by Antonio da San Gallo the Younger, was a massive fortress that perfectly suited the land on which it was set: a small town on the steep slopes of the Cimini hills, overlooking the road from Viterbo to Rome.

Vignola turned Paul III's *Rocca* into a villa for Alessandro Farnese, though he retained the original layout. He died before work was completed, but before he died he designed a summer residence for Farnese, which was to be situated to one side of the palace. Work on the *palazzina* did not begin until 1575, and it was completed around 1586.

Could this be why the overall design of the gardens gives the impression of being incomplete, with the last stages of the visitor's "initiation" missing? The visitor follows the same route as Poliphilus through a dense *bosco* of oak trees to the foot of the magic spring, represented by a water stair bearing sculptures of intertwined dolphins and dominated by a monumental Fountain of the Rivers. Broad semicircular flights of stairs lead down to the first terrace, an enclosed garden of geometric flower beds contained between carefully tended hedges, an evocation of a bygone age. To reach the second terrace, the visitor is again guided

THE GARDEN BECOMES SPECTACLE

Tivoli, Rome
Gardens of the Villa d'Este
ABOVE: Organ Fountain
RIGHT: Water pathway
Francesco Venturini, *Le Fontane dello Giardino Estense in Tivoli*, 1750

by water, this time by the dolphin-shaped fontanelles along the balustrades of the staircases we are meant to follow. There the visitor finds a "garden of pleasance," in contrast to the previous "garden of remembrance." The *palazzina* is exactly between the two gardens, along their axis of symmetry, and opens onto each via a double loggia. One loggia gives a distant view of the garden of remembrance, and the other opens right onto the garden of pleasance. Broad tiers ornamented with basins through which the water pours from one to another lead to a monumental gateway, and it is here that the itinerary through the gardens comes to an abrupt end at the wooded hillside facing the other side of the valley. There is no point of transition, no grotto leading us from the cultivated world of the gardens into the uncultivated world of nature outside.

This sense of incompleteness may be precisely the effect Vignola wanted to create. The moment of initiation was no longer the act of perceiving the natural world and its mysteries gradually revealing themselves, no longer a mixture of desire and fear. Nor was it a deliberate act of artifice designed to enchant the visitor, as it was at Tivoli or Bagnaia. Instead, it was a demonstration of a perfect harmony between art and nature. By the very purity of the way in which the gardens were arranged, this harmony is spontaneously created between the two worlds of the senses and of reason.

After Tivoli, Bagnaia, and Caprarola, moving water became a feature of the many gardens that grew up around Rome. In gardens situated on hillsides, it would be the main guiding force for the visitor. Steps, staircases, and terraces could be used to turn the visitor's path through the gardens into pure spectacle. The vertical itinerary, which the visitor need not necessarily follow, was becoming increasingly common. One of the most spectacular examples was the gardens of Count Garzoni at Collodi, laid out shortly after those at Aldobrandini. In both these gardens, the various stages on the way to initiation begin right at the entrance gate. But before this idea of the garden as spectacle came fully to fruition, architects at the beginning of the seventeenth century were still exploring the idea of initiation.

In 1601 Cardinal Pietro Aldobrandini, the nephew of Pope Clement VIII, asked Giacomo Della Porta to transform the *casina* in the middle of his vineyards at Frascati into a villa. The architect soon realized what scope this steeply sloping area of land offered, with its view extending all the way to Rome. Although there were few natural springs in the area, works were planned on a massive scale to bring water to the gardens and transform them into the water-based fantasy in demand at the time.

But Giacomo Della Porta also saw the gardens as a gradual progression through a series of scenic wonders, allowing the visitor to discover them one by one. A nymphaeum acted as a kind of theater curtain, concealing the beginning of the itinerary but also allowing tantalizing glimpses of it, a kind of staircase of water and light cascading down through dense vegetation. The visitor could reach these gardens only by way of two sets of concealed steps leading down from each side of the terrace on which the nymphaeum was situated. From here, one follows streams and cascades, interspersed with fountains that have now unfortunately disappeared, to the magic grotto, which is more symbolic than tangible. A gushing spring guarded by two grotesque stone figures marks what would be the entrance to the grotto if it existed. The idea of initiation was beginning to be more important than the initiation itself.

Giacomo Della Porta was able to design only the general layout of the villa and its gardens. In 1602 he died of apoplexy on his way back from Frascati. His successors were Carlo Maderno and Giovanni Fontana, who made the itinerary theatrical, where Della Porta had meant it to be more mysterious. They raised the level of the villa and built a loggia on the third floor, which allowed the lord of the manor to survey the entire spectacle at once, including the sight of his guests being sprayed by jets of water concealed in the nymphaeum and fountains. The hydraulic system that operated the water jets was constantly being added to and perfected. In 1621 the cardinal ordered the Frenchman Jacques Sarrazin to sculpt a centaur and a Polyphemus playing a real trumpet and pan pipes.

As with the Villa d'Este, the coffers at the Villa Aldobrandini were empty when the cardinal died. The cost of the sophisticated system of fountains was actually far greater than that of the villa itself. Water had rapidly lost its function of guiding people through the garden and revealing the mysteries of nature in a place where all was harmony and reflectiveness. Increasingly, architects were becoming sorcerer's apprentices, bringing out the magic of the garden to produce visions that delighted the eye only until the novelty wore off.

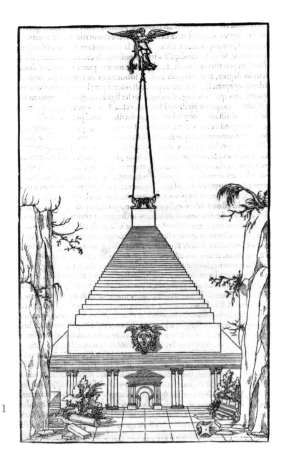

1

In the footstep of Poliphilus,

Here we see the labyrinthine universe *of the garden: the garden is a kind of game, a game deliberately created for the visitor in the manner of a puzzle to be solved, in which the way the rules are presented is more important than the trees and plants from which the game is constructed.*

Abraham Moles, *Labyrinthes du vécu*, 1982

Castello, Florence
Gardens of the Villa Medici, 1538–92
Il Tribolo, Bartolommeo Ammannati,
and Bernardo Buontalenti
Terraces

2

3

Verona, Gardens of the Giusti Palace, begun 1550
Maze, redesigned in the eighteenth century

The first test, the maze . . .

4

OPPOSITE, ABOVE: Pyramidal temple
ABOVE: Poliphilus lost in a dark forest
Francesco Colonna, *Dream of Poliphilus*, 1546

Leaving the maze, the visitor is guided by water—

Tivoli, Rome
Gardens of the Villa d'Este, 1559–72
Alberto Galvani and Pirro Ligorio

BELOW: Girandole, or Dragon Fountain
Pirro Ligorio and T. da Siena
OPPOSITE: Oval Fountain
Pirro Ligorio

1

2

3

The exuberant waters at Tivoli,

Poliphilus quenching his thirst
Francesco Colonna, *Dream of Poliphilus*, 1546

1

The peaceful waters
 at Bagnaia,

2

In the evening of such splendor,
The richness of your presence renders
The age of Florence near once more;

And from the festal cups drifts high
Into the fine and turquoise sky
A soft, smooth dream of strawberries.

Albert Samain, *Le Soir*, 1888

3
Bagnaia, Viterbo
Gardens of the Villa Lante, 1568–98
Designed by Vignola for Cardinal Francesco Gambara, completed for the cardinal of Montalto
OPPOSITE, ABOVE: Giants' Fountain, or Fountain of the Tiber and Arno
OPPOSITE, BELOW: Table of Water
ABOVE: Moorish Fountain, 1589–98

1

Caprarola, Viterbo
Gardens of the Farnese Palazzina, 1575–86
Designed by Vignola
ABOVE: Secret garden
OPPOSITE, ABOVE: Fountain of the Rivers (detail)
OPPOSITE, BELOW: Water Chain, or Dolphins' Fountain

2

3

Frascati, Rome
Gardens of the Villa Aldobrandini, 1601–21
Giacomo Della Porta, Carlo Maderno, and
Giovanni Fontana
ABOVE: Nymphaeum
LEFT: Centaur, 1621
Jacques Sarrazin

Water turns the path through the garden into pure spectacle.

Collodi, Pistoia
Gardens of the Villa Garzoni, begun 1650, designed by Ottavio Diodati
Terraces

Along the path to initiation, heralding the great spectacle of the gardens to come, the elements of nature—earth, air, fire, and water—were revealed to the visitor in the faces of Olympian gods and goddesses, allegories of rivers and mountains, and statues of nymphs, fauns, monsters, or dragons. This stone world was already a feature of the ancient villas around Rome, and princes and patrons from the Renaissance onward commissioned artists to produce catalogs of the statuary and help them form collections of it.

Lorenzo de' Medici was one of the first to do this, ordering the sculptor Bertoldo di Giovanni to bring together the marbles he found in gardens near his palace in the Via Larga. In Rome itself, Pope Julius II needed a suitable site for the statuary he had collected, and the Cortile of the Belvedere, built by Bramante, was the result.

This taste for antique relics spread to courts abroad, and in 1540 Francesco Primaticcio made copies of some of the finest pieces from the Vatican for François I of France: Ariadne, the Belvedere Apollo, the Venus of Cnidus, sphinxes, and satyrs. In all, he made 103 molds, which were taken to Fontainebleau and cast in bronze to ornament the palace. The work was directed by the young Vignola, who went to France with Primaticcio and stayed there until 1543.

In the 1550s, when work was begun on some of the major villas in Rome and the surrounding area, the statue took on a new function that went beyond that of ornament or collector's item. Placed alongside the visitor's route through a garden, it assumed the power conferred on it by the ancients and symbolically revealed nature's hidden mysteries. From being merely background adornment, it took on an important, positive role in the garden.

One of the first to realize the potential of the statue within the overall layout of a garden was the Neapolitan Pirro Ligorio, who built a villa for Cardinal d'Este. Educated at the court of the Carafas, an important family in Naples known for its fine collection of antiques, Ligorio arrived in Rome in 1534 and went to work for some of the prelates who were friends of his former patrons.

In 1542 he was chosen by Pope Paul IV—Gian Petro Carafa—to take part in the restoration of Jules II's collection of marbles at the Cortile of the Belvedere, which had been scattered following the sacking of 1527. Then, in 1550, Vignola asked him to finish the nymphaeum at the Villa Giulia. There he worked with the young Florentine artist Bartolommeo Ammannati. When Ammannati returned to Florence, summoned by the Medicis to continue the work begun by Il Tribolo at Castello and the Boboli Gardens, he carried with him the idea of removing sculpture from its original resting place and using it in a natural setting to bring out the hidden forces of nature.

Pirro Ligorio was given a number of important commissions, and his talents have led some historians to call him the inspiration behind the Sacro Bosco at Bomarzo. It is certainly true that his many contacts in Rome could have introduced him to Vicino Orsini when the young duke commissioned a garden design for his hillside villa at Bomarzo. He wanted a garden that would recall the Arcadia described in the *Dream,* which he knew well through his grandfather Fanciotto Orsini, who had grown up at the court of Lorenzo de' Medici.[11]

The resulting park, "a Sacred Grove beyond compare," comprised a world of "fantastical figures, dug and sculpted straight from the great rocks themselves, symbols sculpted from the stone, mysterious faces, grimacing masks, fabulous animals, all seemingly released by some diabolical force, exalting all that is human and inhuman, the grandeur and the folly of knowledge, the powers of both life and death intermingled."[12] The duke of Bomarzo was spellbound by the gardens and was constantly restoring them. In 1563 he wrote to Alessandro Farnese: "I promise I will have the fountains in my little woods repaired, for they are an affront to the eyes when one walks past them every day."[13] Vicino Orsini had a single passion: talking about his "Bosco" and showing people around it. We know this from his copious letters, and when he went to Florence in 1558 for the wedding of a member of his family, Paolo Orsini, duke of Bracciano, to Isabella de' Medici, he would doubtless have expounded on his project with great enthusiasm.

Francesco de' Medici, Isabella's brother, no doubt had Orsini's enthusiasm in mind when he ordered his architect, Bernardo Buontalenti, Ammannati's successor at the Boboli Gardens, to turn some of his land at Pratolino into a garden that would surpass all others. The piece of land, which was uneven, infertile, and without any natural water, presented a considerable challenge for the architect. Francesco's purpose in building the villa was twofold. First, he wanted to astound his visitors with the technical achievement of his fountains (the cellars of the villa consisted of grottoes containing water-powered automata), and second, he needed

Bomarzo, Viterbo
Sacred Wood, Château Orsini, 1552–84
Dragon being attacked by dogs

a retreat where he could pursue his passionate amours with his mistress, Bianco Capello. And indeed, the duality of this man—the man of the court and the solitary Don Juan—shows clearly in the results of Buontalenti's work.

The new park was much less of a formal, neatly laid out garden than before, consisting of waterfalls and grottoes designed in the spirit of *terribilità*. No longer was the visitor initiated into the inner harmony of nature; instead, the garden revealed unsuspected forces that, had they not been controlled by art and artifice, would have been fearsome. The gardens could be manipulated by their owner to provoke surprise and shock. Once nature could no longer be contained by the world of science, and when the mechanisms controlling the garden eventually broke down, the forces of nature won out over those of man in the gardens at Pratolino. Today, the huge *Apennino* sculpted by Giambologna, drowning in its own melancholy on the edge of a fountain, is the last nostalgic relic of the garden's former glory.

Poliphilus fleeing the dragon
Francesco Colonna, *Dream of Poliphilus*, 1546

THE GROTTO

In 1530 Giulio Romano put the finishing touches to the Palazzo del Té in Mantova, which he had built for Frederick II, duke of Gonzaga. As part of the Cortile, Romano built a *casino della grotta,* decorated with stucco and seashells. After 1530, "for a century and longer, no garden or residence was complete without one of these structures, which showed the dwelling as part of the surrounding countryside and nature in the service of pleasure and ostentation."[14]

The grotto, a place of quiet coolness and relaxation, became an essential design element in the decoration of the garden, but equally essential, it became a stage on the road to initiation. It was here that the fearsome mystery of the Creation was revealed, the alchemy of fire and water, in the spring, which has its source within the grotto, and through the rays of sunlight that filter into it.

We have seen how for the Cretans the grotto was an integral part of the trial of the labyrinth. Over the centuries it functioned in turn as the gate to hell, the home of evil giants, and the refuge of gods and nymphs. Poliphilus himself wondered whether the cave he had crept into to escape a fiery dragon was not the hollow rock where the cruel Cyclops Polyphemus lived, or perhaps the cavern of the evil Cacus, son of Vulcan.

Using the *Dream* as a guide in designing their gardens, the Medicis naturally wanted to include a grotto in each garden. At Castello, Il Tribolo had placed sculptures of animals from the Nile under a vault of stucco, shells, and pebbles; these animals, according to Ovid, were the first to inhabit the Earth. The figures were sculpted by Giacomo Fancelli, a pupil of the court sculptor Bandinelli. By turning the story of Creation into theater, the mystery of the birth of nature could be revealed.

Bernardo Buontalenti, Francesco de' Medici's tutor and organizer of the feasts and other events that took place at the Uffizi, produced a design for the Boboli Gardens on the same theme in 1583. The first in the series of tableaux showed the Earth being born out of chaos before the Deluge; the Florentine artist Bernardino Poccetti filled the scene with wild animals and thick undergrowth.

Superimposed on this slightly disquieting world was a bucolic vision in stucco and chalk stones of shepherds tending their flocks under the troubled gaze of the river gods and nymphs. This Arcadian world was about to come to an end. In the center, on the basin of a fountain, was a simple mossy rock. This, and the whole scene, symbolized the world as it was between the Creation and the Fall: the original state of matter, which was the source of energy both positive and destructive. The scene enclosed the intertwined figures of Theseus and Helen. Originally this was to have been Pyrhha and Deucalion, who, according to Ovid, were the only two human beings to survive the Flood. Behind them was a second tableau, the *Grotticella*. At its center, four fauns attended the birth of Venus, a graceful white marble piece by Giambologna showing the goddess sheltering beneath a *trompe l'oeil* arbor of flowers and birds set off with inlaid stones and mosaics. Every morning for about an hour, Venus was reborn as the rays of the sun filtered through the *oculus* in the ceiling.

Gradually and imperceptibly the grotto, like the garden itself, gained in fascination. The myth of Orpheus became less tragic; the poet no longer descended into the underworld in search of Eurydice. Instead, he stayed near the entrance and enchanted with his music not only the birds and animals but also the guests of the garden's owner. Nymphs gave way to Muses, who could initiate the visitor into the power of poetry, music, and dance. To these diversions were soon added the rather more malicious pleasures in which the courts of seventeenth century Europe indulged.

Castello, Florence
Gardens of the Villa Medici, 1538–92
Apennius, c. 1550
Bartolommeo Ammannati

"After crossing the waves, the boat will arrive at the Isolotto, and the pilgrim will be able to pluck the golden fruits of Fortune from the branches of the orange trees. This will be his reward for leading a temperate life."[15] This is the final stage along the path to initiation, celebrating the visitor's joy on surmounting various obstacles along the way to have the natural order of things at last revealed to him. He has now acquired Knowledge, as Poliphilus found Polia. It can be seen in two great gardens designed almost half a century apart.

The first of these is again to be found in the Boboli Gardens in Florence. In 1608 Cosimo II had just married Maria Magdalena of Austria, a rich heiress of the Hapsburg family. He now appointed Giulio Parigi, the great-nephew of the sculptor Bartolommeo Ammannati, and his son, Alfonso, as chief architects for the gardens. The grand duke gave his architects a number of important improvements to carry out. Giulio Parigi was to transform the green area designed by Ammannati in front of the palace into a huge amphitheater, in which a row of niches at the end of each terrace would contain statues of the Olympian gods and give the amphitheater a classical grandeur. Alfonso was to extend the gardens eastward toward the Porta Romana and create a *teatro maritimo* along the lines of the naumachia of the Villa Adriana.

Alfonso Parigi designed a long, steeply sloping avenue to enhance the theatrical effect of the whole and create an element of surprise by leaving the visitor to guess

THE APPROACH TO THE ISLAND OF CYTHERA

what would happen next. Tall hedges lined each side of the path, planted in alternate rows and concealing the marble figures of gods and goddesses, which formed an important part of the total effect. A century later, these hedges were replaced with dark cypresses. The path finally opened onto a wide oval basin, and in the middle of a little island was the Isolotto, covered in orange and lemon trees. The ocean was accompanied by the three great rivers: the Nile, the Ganges, and the Euphrates. To produce this result, Alfonso Parigi moved and raised Giambologna's fountain, originally sculpted to mark the beginning of the gardens opposite the Pitti Palace.

Two bridges made it look as though the "golden fruits" were easy to reach, but there were high portals topped with ibexes, which formed part of the Medici family crest, and guarded by sea monsters to keep the unwanted visitor away. The visitor was thus a spectator, with no role to play in the overall design; he could go no further than the edge of the basin, but here he will see "Andromeda, as graceful as Venus herself, offering her face to the light with a gesture of her upraised arm and awaiting the arrival of Perseus"[16] The erotic tension of this scene was reminiscent of another, identical one that the visitor briefly glimpsed at the *Grotticella*.

The Isolotto heralded both the beginning of the seventeenth century and the advent of the great architecture of the baroque period. The gardens of Isola Bella on Lake Maggiore were the pinnacle of this new trend in Italy, but even more important, they pushed the relationship between man and nature to the limits of the realms of possibility; here man was held back, kept away from what was essentially an inaccessible dream seen from afar on a little island in the middle of a lake, which, on a misty day, was virtually invisible.

Work began on the gardens at Isola Bella shortly after the completion of Cosimo II's Isolotto; the *teatro maritimo* was not finished until 1618. But at Isola Bella, work went on for fifty years and still the original project was not completed. Giulio Cesare Borromea, a member of the famous family of Cardinal Carlo Borromea, began work on the palace and gardens, and it was Charles III and Vitaliano VI who brought it to its current state. He gave Antonio Crivelli and his architects the job of transforming the arid islet, which was almost totally devoid of vegetation—practically a lump of rock—and bore only a few poverty-stricken fishermen's houses. It was to become "worthy of the fairies who seem to have brought part of the ancient garden of the Hesperides to this spot."[17]

Isola Bella, an abbreviated form of Isola Isabella, named after Charles III's beautiful and much-adored Isabella d'Adda, offers itself without reservation to the visitor, like the island of Cythera in the *Dream:* "A place so beautiful, pleasant, and delectable that even the most eloquent language would not be rich enough to describe it if it chose to do so."[18]

There were other similarities between the gardens of Borromea and the island of Cythera. Both had the same highly geometrical design, a series of concentric shapes outlined by hedges of low bushes, a kind of false labyrinth, which was circular on Cythera and rectangular at Isola Bella. But on the island in Lake Maggiore, the hedges and colonnades of balusters formed a maze only when viewed from above. In fact, they marked the edges of ten broad terraces sweeping upward from the lake. At the apex of this great pyramid, an outdoor theater was bordered on one side by the back of a huge nymphaeum, which formed the northern boundary of the gardens. From the top of this nymphaeum, which was also pyramidal, with three superimposed orders, the unicorn, the emblem of the Borromea family, reared upward.

There were other nymphaea on the terraces and basins and among the flower beds, where flowers planted in the eighteenth century and afterward—camellias, arbutuses, tamarisks, and soapwort—mingled their scents with the roses and jasmine that Vitaliano had planted.

These gardens seem almost to have risen from the depths of the water. They are a marvelous accompaniment along the path to initiation, but they also mark its end. There is no better illustration of this quest for knowledge, symbolized by the purity of the unicorn, the sublimation of the spirit. But the unicorn in the nymphaeum at Isola Bella is being ridden by Eros, the son of Venus, goddess of physical beauty. On each terrace, as on the island of Cythera, the visitor's senses are so overcome by the perfume of the flowers, the music of the fountains, and the visual beauty of the lake that he forgets he has reached the end of the path to initiation, the conquest of knowledge. Now, like Poliphilus at the end of his dream, he can satisfy his desires in pure pleasure. He has finally realized that what these gardens really reveal, like the *Dream,* is "no more than initiation into the mysteries of Venus."[19]

The forces of nature, guardian of the grotto . . .

Pratolino, Florence
Gardens of the Villa Francesco de' Medici, 1569–87
Apennius, 1569–81
Giambologna

1

2

Bomarzo, Viterbo
Sacred Wood, Château Orsini, 1552–84
Tortoise bearing the Winged Victory

3

Frascati, Rome
Gardens of the Villa Aldobrandini, 1601–21
Giacomo Della Porta, Carlo Maderno, and
Giovanni Fontana
Figure of a monster, 1612

Castello, Florence
Gardens of the Villa Medici, 1538–92
The grotto
Decorated by Il Tribolo
Nile animals attributed to Giovanni Paolo Fancelli

Fabulous animals in the grotto of Castello . . .

Boboli Gardens, Florence
The grotto, 1583
Bernardo Buontalenti
ABOVE AND RIGHT: First hall
Fresco and stucco decoration by Bernardo
Poccetti
OPPOSITE: The Grotticella
Venus leaving her bath, c. 1580–87
Giambologna

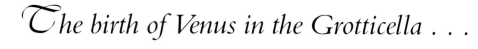

The path toward initiation . . .

1

2

3

4

$\mathcal{A}t$ the Isolotto . . .

Boboli Gardens, Florence
The Isolotto, completed 1618
Alfonso Parigi
OPPOSITE, ABOVE: Avenue of cypresses
leading to the Isolotto
OPPOSITE, BELOW: Ocean Fountain, 1570–76
Giambologna
ABOVE: Perseus
Attributed to Giambologna
LEFT: Andromedea
School of Giambologna

1

Isola Bella, Lake Maggiore
Gardens of the Borromea Palace, 1620–71
Built for Charles III and his son, Vitaliano VI
Angelo Crivelli and Pietro Antonio Barca
ABOVE: Terraces
RIGHT: Nymphaeum
OPPOSITE: Isola Bella seen from the lakeside,
early morning

2

At Isola Bella

3

Polia and myself, united in our desires, both wishing to attain that place set aside for our beatitude, and sighing softly with ardent love, arrived at the port of the holy island of Cythera in Cupid's boat.

Francesco Colonna, *Dream of Poliphilus*, 1546

THE PATH TO KNOWLEDGE

*Italy and France
from the Fifteenth
to the Seventeenth
Century*

uring his voyage through the land of dreams in search of Polia, Poliphilus undergoes experiences that reveal how this dream world functions. He is confronted by the forces of nature and initiated into the mysteries of Creation, but first he has to decode the remains left behind by ancient cultures so that he can understand their message.

Before the initiation can take place, he still has two secret gardens to discover: the *glass garden*, which reveals the world of reason to Poliphilus, and the *silk garden*, which reveals the world of the senses. Both gardens contain all of nature's resources, not only those man can put to use but also those that give him aesthetic pleasure.

Poliphilus is led to the gardens by two nymphs. Logistica, the first, shows him the glass garden, "a meadow where the trunks and branches of the trees are made of fine gold, but the leaves are made of glass, so perfect that they look exactly like real ones. Likewise there are grass and flowers made of glass, of various colors, forms, and species. The garden is enclosed by bulbous columns made of glass or jasper, covered in the herb called bindweed, with white bell-shaped flowers colored exactly as they are in nature."[1]

In this garden all is transparent, offering man all the benefits he can obtain from nature and teaching him laws to which he can apply his intelligence and formulate more laws. This first example is the garden of "simples," or medicinal herbs. The next is the *botanical garden*, which opens the door to knowledge not only of the natural sciences but also of other sciences, ranging from chemistry to medicine. In the glass garden we also find the *utility garden*, which, although its main purpose is profit, shows the same geometrical composition and the same mastery of garden design.

After his visit to the glass garden under the guidance of Logistica, Poliphilus is taken by Thelemia to the garden of silk, a garden

> no less pleasing to behold than the garden shown to him by Logistica. . . . This garden is the same size, and laid out in the same way as the glass garden, except that the flowers, trees, and grasses in it are made of silk. . . . The walls of this garden have been built with great industry, and at incredible expense. They are collections of pearls across which has been woven a stem of ivy with leaves of silk, its branches of fine gold and grapes made from precious stones. . . . The flower beds are covered in green velvet and look like a beautiful pasture in early April. . . . Thelemia took her lyre and joined its sound with that of her voice to sing of how these delights first began.[2]

These delights could not remain exclusive to Poliphilus. Soon, the *garden of pleasance* began to appear alongside the utility garden, and soon poets, artists, and nobles would have lawns as velvety and flowers and plants as precious as those Poliphilus found in the garden of silk. The expenditure would be far less extravagant, but the garden of pleasance soon became a necessary ornament to any princely dwelling.

The visitor has now undergone a series of revelations modeled on the *Dream*, leading him eventually to view nature in a different way. He could see the garden as a place of privileged experience, where sensations buried in the depths of his soul could rise to the surface. This process of initiation prepared him to receive knowledge: Now he could understand that everything revolved around the silk garden and the glass garden. As Logistica and Thelemia showed Poliphilus, the visitor had to recognize his dependence on the benefits the soil brought and experience the pleasure they provided before such a garden could be created. He had to conquer nature, but only in the name of Order and Beauty.

The garden used for growing medicinal herbs gave birth in turn to the botanical garden, the archetype of a garden of knowledge. More than any other type of garden, this allowed access to the world of science as revealed through the secrets of the plants. But the botanical garden itself had a utilitarian as well as a revelatory function: It was a necessary part of everyday life. Until the end of the sixteenth century, many recommendations were written as to how it should be planted and laid out.

The botanical garden was thus inevitably associated with the silk garden so dear to Francesco Colonna. Paradoxically, as people paid more attention to the

Frascati, Rome
Gardens of the Villa Aldobrandini, 1601–21
Giacomo Della Porta, Carlo Maderno, and
Giovanni Fontana
Nymphaeum, statue of Polyphemus, 1621

idea of the garden for profit, its opposite, the garden for pleasure with no utilitarian function, came into being and gradually replaced it. But before these two opposite functions were divided, utility and aesthetic pleasure were combined in the design of that rare refuge from the troubles of the world—the medieval monastery garden. The classical tradition of the garden as a series of enclosed spaces, each serving a precise function, was preserved during the first troubled centuries of Christianity.

From the ninth century onward, monasteries were reorganizing and multiplying amid vast areas of agricultural land and allocating a particular function to each part of their grounds. There were generally three separate areas, each fulfilling a need of the monastery's inhabitants. First, there was the "simples" garden, where medicinal plants were grown alongside flowers used to decorate the altars of the chapel. Then there was the kitchen garden, used for growing small vegetables. Both types were divided into regular rectangular strips of earth, slightly raised and separated either by planks of wood, low walls, or trellises. This practice continued into the seventeenth century. The third area was perhaps the most important from a symbolic point of view, the orchard. Here plants were grown for the pleasure they gave: Hawthorn, rosebushes, and honeysuckle grew alongside fruit trees on a carpet of green grass. It was a place of relaxation and repose (the monks were buried there when they died), a revelation of eternity, and from the thirteenth century onward the orchard gave its name to a collection of gardens, each having a clearly defined function.

Gardens continued to follow the monastic scheme, but their organization—and not simply the elements of their design—began to interest scholars. In his *De Vegetabilibus*, written about 1230, the Dominican Albert de Bollstaedt went beyond merely cataloging all the known plants and wrote for the first time about the layout of gardens. But the first person to treat the "art of gardens" in any depth was the agronomist Pietro de' Crescenzi. His work, *Opus ruralium commodorum*, written between 1304 and 1309, met with such success that after 1350 it was written in the vernacular and in 1373 translated into French as *Rustican du labeur des champs*. In later editions, after 1483, it was retitled *Livre des prouffits champestres et ruraux*.[3]

GARDENS OF EDEN, COURTLY PASTURES

Master of the Central Rhine
Garden of Eden
Distemper, c. 1420

These translations were a major factor in the transition from gardens solely as objects of utility, tended by monks with a passion for botany, to pleasure gardens built for princes. Contact with the Arab world during the Crusades also hastened this transition, for the Arabs had already discovered the pleasures that nature in the service of man could bring. Pietro de' Crescenzi was the first to describe this new function of the garden. In his *Opus ruralium* he devoted a whole chapter to what he called "orchards, gardens, and places of pleasure. And trees, herbs, and fruits. How they should be arranged in artistic fashion . . ."⁴ He also classified them in accordance with the type of person he would expect to use them. Thus the orchard became the home of everything that was grown for pleasure: fruit trees, aromatic herbs, flowers, and, by extension, those places where man's enjoyment of nature was heightened. In this chapter Crescenzi suggests three categories of "orchards": "small orchards," "orchards for persons of some standing," and "royal orchards."

Small orchards contain herbs and fruit trees and allow their owners, generally of modest means, to benefit from the pleasures nature has to offer. A meadow, with tightly packed squares of herbs "like a sheet of green," is surrounded by aromatic herbs and grasses and flowers. On one side of the garden there is a bank of greenery, two low walls enclosing an area of turf, which invites the visitor to repose. A trellis, or perhaps a small arbor covered in vines, provides protection from the sun.

The second category of orchard is similar to the first described by Crescenzi but larger. It is situated near the villa of a rich merchant or noble, its gardens divided into a number of areas separated by hedges and containing a wide variety of plants and trees. Here the orchard is ornamented not with simple banks of greenery but with trellises, bowers, and trellised pavilions on which plants could be grown. The trellised pavilion was common until the end of the sixteenth century.

Oriande and Maugis seated in garden
Renaud de Montauban, *Les Amours de Maugis et Oriande*, 1460

The pleasures found in these gardens were even more in evidence in orchards for royalty and other powerful and rich nobles. Here the garden was again divided into several areas, each serving one of the pleasures enjoyed by the nobles of the day: woods for hunting, lakes, and aviaries for game birds and songbirds. The construction of woods was itself becoming more sophisticated. A wood was now a "palace" made from the branches of cherry or apple trees or hazel boughs.

Despite Crescenzi's recommendations, the pleasure garden remained integrated with the utility garden. Essentially it was becoming more and more a place that had the power to evoke certain emotions, and in courtly romance the enclosed garden is an important feature, for it allows those who enter to experience rare and complex emotions created by the plants that grow in the garden. This romantic orchard, with its fruit and flowers with evocative Oriental names, banks of grass, where lovers take their repose, and a fountain (often the Fountain of Youth), served as the backdrop to many thirteenth- and fourteenth-century poems and *fabliaux*. The model for all these works was the *Roman de la Rose*, where the Lover seeks to possess the object of his love—the Rose—in the Garden of Delights.⁵

Around this time, the garden became a source of inspiration for religious art. Artists from northern Europe—Alsace, Germany, and Flanders—used gardens as a background for their portrayals of the Madonna and Child.⁶ The orchard symbolized the pure emotions of courtly love: Woman surrounded by religious veneration with the *hortus conclusus* recalling Mary's own virgin purity, "a garden inclosed . . . a spring shut up."⁷ Both romantic and religious love can be expressed in the same "inward-looking idea of a nature that is exquisite, pure, paradisiacal, given over to the ineffable joys of the soul."⁸

This poetic, symbolic vision became reality in Tuscany at the end of the fifteenth century, when princes were beginning to build villas outside the walls of the town and philosophers and poets were beginning to find renewed inspiration in nature. Another factor, perhaps less obvious but nonetheless important, underlined the break between what was useful and what was pleasant. The gradual decline of the courtly garden as a symbol of all that was inaccessible into a place where more sensual pleasures could be enjoyed was partly a result of the influence of Neoplatonism on the court of the Medicis, but also partly a result of the many contacts the court had with the Middle East. Scholars from Greece and Asia Minor were welcomed in Florence, for even if their cultures were rooted in Greek or Roman antiquity, they were also clearly affected by their relationships with the Arab world.[9]

So the *giardino segreto*, one of the three gardens that were starting to be built for the many new villas springing up in Florence and Lucca, had its roots not only in the monastery garden (the main feature it borrowed being the high walls that shut it off from the outside) but also in the Middle East. For example, it included flower beds laid out in intricate designs, each kept distinct from its neighbors through the varied use of aromatic plants. There was the same Middle Eastern predilection for the cypress tree, and also for the rose, with its overtones of love. But above all, it had the same purpose: The secret garden was a place of delights that gave pleasure to the senses and tranquillity to the body and mind.

The few examples of *giardini segreto* still accessible in Tuscany—those of the Villa Capponi, the Villa Santini-Torrigiani, and the Villa Gamberaia—are not perfect examples of this type of garden, for each passing century has brought new changes to their layout. However, the garden of the Villa Capponi, situated on the hills overlooking Florence, perhaps best retains the original charm these enclosed spaces held, even though it was not designed until 1572. It is a small garden with high walls, slightly below the level of the villa and thus invisible and inaccessible from the villa itself. An underground passage leads into the garden from inside the building. Here, even today, beds of mauve silenes (probably originally roses and jasmine) with immaculately cut borders are surrounded by high walls covered in climbing plants, such as roses and wisteria. In one of these walls is an opening with a grille, through which Florence and the dome of Santa Maria dei Fiori are visible in the distance. This opening has a symbolic function: It allows the spirit to wander where it will, while still serving as a reminder that one is kept in by the walls of this oasis of greenery, shielded from the wind and kept warm by the sunlit stones so that the perfumes of the flowers are experienced with even more intensity.

The *giardino segreto* is not the only feature of the Tuscan villa garden. In front of the villa is an open field reserved for games and festivities. On one side, near the entrance gate, the *orto* allows the cultivation of vegetables and aromatic herbs, and orange and lemon trees in earthenware pots intermingle with beds of vegetables. It is thus a trio of gardens, serving as a place of quiet meditation, noisy celebration, and functional utility. Something of the sort is also found in the conversions of the villas at Cafaggiolo and Careggi into pleasure gardens, which Michelozzo undertook for Cosimo the Elder. But first and foremost it was his brother, Lorenzo, who gave these gardens their sensual beauty, for it conformed with his poet's sensibilities and acted at his inspiration. Like his friend the poet Angelo Poliziano, whose Island of Venus in the *Stanzas* is full of the voluptuous luxury of the Medicis, Lorenzo loved to immerse himself in the shimmering colors and subtle odors of the gardens at Careggi, for they were "a veritable fairyland of different aromas."[10]

This modest-size Tuscan pleasure garden was included in many of the great gardens of the Medici during the sixteenth century. At Castello, Il Tribolo built a medicinal herb garden, a glass garden to the left of the villa, and a silk garden with a pavilion made of foliage and working models of birds to its right, both enclosed and to one side of the great succession of terraces that make up the garden. Unfortunately, these were destroyed when the garden was refurbished in the eighteenth century.

In France, kings and lords did not wait until the Italian wars and the beginning of the sixteenth century to enjoy the pleasures of the silk garden. Poets had already initiated the courts into the subtle pleasures of chaste love in gardens that were eternally in bloom.

Although the small garden, serving as both a place of pleasure and of utility, was widespread throughout the Middle Ages—the charters of the main towns show that there were many hidden away behind the walls of the merchant classes—

THE "GIARDINO SEGRETO" OF TUSCANY

Pietro de' Crescenzi, *Rustican du labeur des champs*, 1373
Illuminated manuscript translated into French by order of Charles V

THE ROYAL PLEASURES IN FRANCE

it was rare for such a garden to be built on a royal scale along the lines of those built by Crescenzi. Three main examples mark the point of transition between this period, when the feudal castle contained a few small pleasances within its ramparts, and the end of the fifteenth century, when the orchard of courtly romance had been elevated to the status of ornamental garden.

At Hesdin, near Arras in the Pas de Calais, in 1289, Robert II of Artois returned from a long stay in Naples as regent of the kingdom of Sicily. He brought with him a number of books on mechanics and hydraulics that had been written for him. He had discovered these sciences from Arab manuscripts (in particular, those of Banu-Mouza and Al-Jazari)[11] he found in the royal libraries during his stay in Naples. He pictured the construction of a *parc de joyeusetés* near his château that would contain automata and trick fountains—"engins pour mouiller les dames"—to surprise and frighten guests.[12] This it continued to do until the area was razed by the troops of Charles V in 1553.

Almost fifty years after Robert II's park had been built, the gardens of the Hôtel Saint-Pol, Charles V's favorite residence in Paris, began to attract widespread admiration. Built between 1360 and 1418, they were not simply collections of fountains and jets of water but an ingenious arrangement of countless promenades, galleries, arbors, and pavilions. This trellis architecture was fragile and short-lived, but it became a popular feature of princes' gardens.

After the introduction of water-powered automata (which did not reappear until the seventeenth century) and the ephemeral architecture of Saint-Pol came a more durable form of garden.

René d'Anjou was fascinated by gardening, and after a long stay in Naples, from which he was expelled by Alphonse d'Aragon in 1442, he had a large number of gardens built at the gates of Angers and on his lands along the river Loire. But more important, he wanted to turn the medieval orchard into a royal garden and introduced the *jardin de singularités*, already widespread in the Islamic world where princes would ask their gardeners to create unusual grafts and cut plants and hedges in unusual ways. The French adopted this new fashion, and the *jardin de singularités* rapidly became an art form at which the French excelled.

King René thus brought a new mode of gardening back from Italy. Fifty years later, when Charles VIII returned from his Italian campaign in 1495, he brought with him a new way of life, in which gardens assumed another new dimension. The king had been particularly impressed by the residence of the Aragons in Naples, Poggio Reale, with its broad avenues, rose beds, and water everywhere one looked. He brought back about twenty artists and workers, a gardener who was experienced in the science of hydraulics, Dom Pacello di Mercogliano, and an architect and engineer, Fra Giocondo. Charles VIII was very much aware of the importance of creating a setting for his court befitting his royal policies, in which diplomacy played an increasingly important part. This meant that the pleasure garden was a necessity not only as a diversion for visiting lords and ladies but also to enhance his own prestige. The garden might retain its fortresslike appearance, with its enclosing walls and moats, but its function was purely a decorative one.

This new role assumed by the garden did not mean that it was totally redesigned. It continued to conform to existing rules, and even though châteaux were no longer shut up against the outside world and now had many outbuildings and gardens, these were still kept just outside the walls, separate from the buildings themselves.

Pacello da Mercogliano's first experiments on French soil were at Amboise, but it was not until he was summoned to Blois by Louis XII following the death of the king's father that he was able to make full use of his art. Between 1500 and 1510 he planted the gardens, still beyond the moat, in three huge terraces arranged in a way that was quite new to this age.

The first garden, known as the Jardin de la Bretonnerie, named after one of the former gardens of the old château, was laid out fairly simply. A gallery above the orangery led to the second terrace, where a showpiece pleasance was created. Because of its new role, the garden could be reached directly from the château. A wooden gallery, the Galerie des Cerfs, splendidly decorated with hunting trophies, led the king and queen straight from the royal apartments into the garden.

The outside of the gardens was marked by a path covered by a trellis bearing climbing plants. On one side, the path became an enclosed passage, leading to a small hexagonal chapel, the oratory of Anne of Brittany, Louis XII's wife. In the middle of the terrace, which was divided into ten squares, a wooden pavilion, linked by arbors to the lateral paths, contained a white marble fountain with three basins placed one atop another. The fountain was richly ornamented and the Italian

The king and his "jardin de singularités"
René d'Anjou, *Le Mortifiement de vaine plaisance*, 1455

The glass garden

1

Botanical gardens, Padua, 1545
Created by Francesco Bonafede, an herbal doctor

2
Arcetri, Florence
Gardens of the Villa Capponi, 1572
Orto, or utility garden

From the botanical garden to the "garden for profit"

The silk garden

O Garden where the trellised vine
Joineth with the shady bower;
In little Eden's garden find
The place where Venus and her kind
Discuss the finer points of love
And where Cupid stalks around,
His piercing arrows in his hand.

Gilles Corrozet, *Blason du jardin*, 1550

3

From the pleasure garden to the secret garden

OPPOSITE, ABOVE: Secret garden
RIGHT: Poliphilus and Polia beneath an arbor
Francesco Colonna, *Dream of Poliphilus*, 1546

Arcetri, Florence
Gardens of the Villa Capponi, 1572
ABOVE AND OPPOSITE, BELOW: *Giardino segreto*

4

Italy brought to the banks of the Loire

Château de Villandry, Indre et Loire
Gardens designed for Jean le Breton, begun 1536, restored 1906 onward
ABOVE AND OPPOSITE, BELOW: Ornamental and utility gardens

OPPOSITE, ABOVE: Elevation of the gardens at Blois
Jacques Androuet Du Cerceau, *Les Plus Excellents Bastiments de France*, 1576–79

1

An ornamental garden and a utility garden side by side

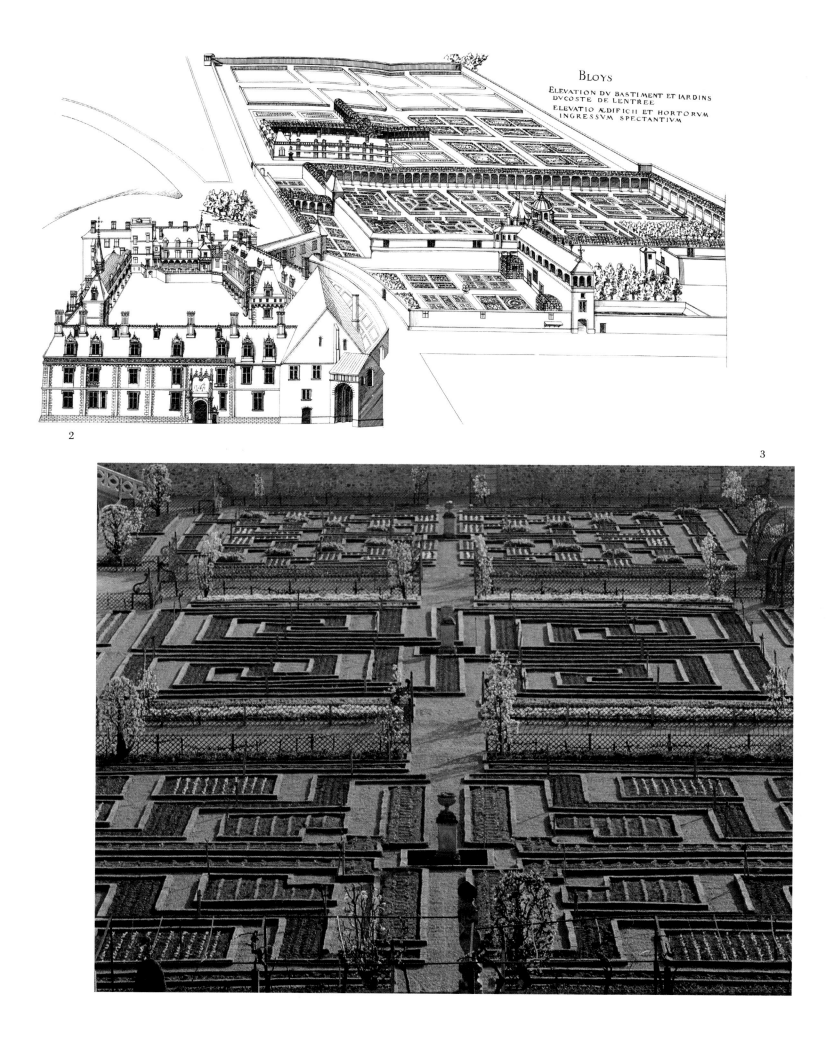

BLOYS

ELEVATION DV BASTIMENT ET IARDINS
DV COSTE DE L'ENTREE
ELEVATIO ÆDIFICII ET HORTORVM
INGRESSVM SPECTANTIVM

2

3

LA FONTAINE OVES LA FIGVRE DE LA
DIANE.
FONS SVPERQVO EST SIMVLACRVM
DIANÆ

The enclosed gardens of Diana . . .

O, thou who art the sovereign virgin,
O nymph, O goddess,
But goddess above all thou seemest,
If goddess thou art, perhaps thou art my Diana,
Whoever thou art, mortal even, open thyself to me.

Angelo Poliziano, *Stanze per la Giostra*, 1478

Fountain of Diana for the courtyard of Château d'Anet
Jacques Androuet Du Cerceau,
Les Plus Excellents Bastiments de France, 1576–79

1

2

3

Château de Raray, Oise
Courtyard and gardens rebuilt by Nicolas de Lancy, c. 1600
OPPOSITE, BELOW: False portico separating the courtyard and gardens
ABOVE: Red Gate, or Diana's Gate

The new flower beds no longer offered the sensual pleasures of the silk garden, with their somewhat cold geometry and princely formality. The only place where these pleasures could be found was in the grotto or nymphaeum, designed to excite all the visitor's senses through the music of water, the coolness of rock, and the shimmering seashell decorations and their smell of the sea. The grotto was an important stage on the path to initiation. But gradually it changed from being a mysterious place of refuge, full of symbols, which one entered with a certain amount of trepidation, to a place of enchantment, where many natural objects were used to create a wholly unnatural setting, with stucco stalactites, shells, and crystals interspersed with *trompe l'oeil* frescoes. The grottoes were still inhabited by gods and goddesses, fauns and nymphs, but their function was now that of imbuing the grotto with a feeling of sacredness. They became part of a permanent spectacle of ingenious fountains and water jets.

Nymphs were a particularly popular feature of these grottoes, and often the word "grotto," with its slightly somber connotations, was replaced by "nymphaeum." Even in antiquity, Roman patricians liked to fill their gardens with nymphs; they were the goddesses of the hidden waters who made nature fertile and aroused a mixture of veneration and fear. The springs they inhabited were a symbol both of life itself and of Genius, or Knowledge, and their altars were dedicated both to Amalthea, the nymph who nursed Zeus, and Egeria, the source of inspiration. These refuges, with their slightly unnerving coolness, were often more fascinating than frightening, for the nymphs also symbolized the idea of "heroic folly," which led to the greatest exploits in love and war. So the nymphaea became places of rest and pleasure, and they were built not only in gardens but also in palaces and public baths.

From the mid-sixteenth century onward, the artists of Florence and Rome drew on this theme. Whether the nymphaeum was constructed in the basement of a building or on a garden terrace, it soon either became a small building on its own or had a facade so richly decorated that it stood out clearly from the buildings around it. Inside were one or more grottoes, and water was omnipresent. In fact, water was so important that the nymphaeum could also by extension be a monumental fountain, a kind of theater of water reflected in a large basin. It no longer contained a grotto, but the sculptures of river gods or pieces of rock attached to the building that gave it a rustic, rough-hewn look were reminiscent of a grotto.

After peace returned to Rome following the sack of 1527, Pope Julius II and Pope Pius IV both requested their architects and sculptors to design nymphaea for the resplendent villas they built near the Vatican gardens. Nor was the court of Rome the only place where these allusions to a distant Arcadia were popular. Francis I, who was even more dazzled than his father by the splendors of Italy, had gods, goddesses, and nymphs made for many of his gardens and palaces in France, particularly Fontainebleau. In 1543 he ordered his favorite artist, Primaticcio, to create a grotto in a small pavilion that formed part of the château and opened directly onto the Jardin des Pins. Here, the artist built "a nymphs' retreat whose stucco interior is decorated with shells and mosaics; Juno and Minerva preside over the whole, from the fresco on the ceiling to the complex fantasies of the central basin."[18]

The courtiers whom the king sent in ever-increasing numbers to represent him at the Holy See were also taken with the splendor of the palaces of Rome. One of these, Claude d'Urfé, returned to his lands at Forez, near Lyon, in 1553 and began transforming the Bastie built by his forefathers into a manor in the style of the day. This inevitably included a grotto, or *salle de fraîcheur*, which was created inside the actual building rather than in the gardens. In this nymphaeum, a whole world of *rocaille*, almost certainly inspired by the engravings of Augustino Veneziano, stands out against a base of stucco stalactites and pebble mosaics. Basins placed in small vaulted niches and carefully placed jets of water give the nymphaeum its cool feeling. The figures of nymphs and satyrs combine to excite the visitor's senses, while Claude d'Urfé, who is depicted on one of the walls, looks on coldly. He knows that to enter the chapel, the refuge of the spirit, situated in front of the nymphaeum, he must first know the world of the senses. All this makes it clear that the lord of the manor at Urfé was not unfamiliar with the *Dream of Poliphilus*, which was published in French in 1546.

The idea of the nymphaeum originated in the ancient gardens of Rome, and did not fully catch on in France until the Medicis came to the ascendancy. When Henry II died in 1559, his wife, Catherine de' Medici, decided to make the gardens of his châteaux at Chenonceaux and the Tuileries into a setting worthy of the kind of festivities that took place in her own country. Inevitably, these were to include the nymphaeum and the grotto.

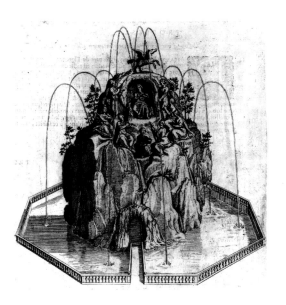

In the same year, the feasts celebrating the marriage of Catherine's daughter to Charles, duke of Lorraine, had taken place amid the grandeur of Primaticcio's gardens of the Château de Meudon. This was more a palace of nymphs than a simple nymphaeum, where the architecture combined to celebrate "a kind of pastoral feast, with the nostalgic imagery of an ancient Arcadia"[19] against a background of walls shimmering with shell designs, coral, majolica, and enameled arabesques.

To make these grottoes even more attractive, the queen invited the Huguenot scholar, Bernard Palissy, who was a potter and enameler, to come and work for her. The work created by this craftsman, who had discovered the secret of Italian enameling, reminded her of the palaces of her childhood. In 1563 Palissy published a treatise, *Recepte véritable*, and two years later received a commission for a decorated grotto for the Tuileries gardens to be added to various other amusements, such as a zoo and an aviary. Palissy produced a grotto similar to the one he had built at the Château d'Ecouen for Anne de Montmorency. Henry II and Diane de Poitiers

OPPOSITE: Drawing of a Mount Parnassus where several grottoes may be built
ABOVE: Drawing of a fountain using a human figure to represent a river
Salomon de Caus, *La Raison des Forces Mouvantes*, 1615

borrowed the house in 1535 as a place to conduct their affair, which at the time was still platonic. Among other things, they found a small room whose windows were decorated with stunning erotic pictures.

Although his work no longer exists, Palissy describes the grotto at Ecouen in his *Architecture et ordonnance de la grotte rustique* and clearly evokes what the atmosphere inside must have been like: "All manner of aquatic plants and mosses grow on a strangely shaped rock, and there are also countless animals and reptiles. . . . Some crawl in one direction, and others cross their path at right angles, many of them making movements in imitation of nature."[20] The animals, powered by water, were made of enameled pottery, as were the fruits and seashells that surrounded them.

After Palissy fell from grace when his patroness died, he was imprisoned in the Bastille for his religious beliefs and died a year later, in 1590. By now these strange decorations were no longer found in grottoes, but they lost none of their fascination. Indeed, they had become even more popular by the time Henry IV returned from Italy. It was he who appointed Etienne Du Pérac his chief royal architect. Du Pérac was a great admirer of the papal villas, and under his direction the gardens of the new royal residence, Saint-Germain-en-Laye, were totally redesigned in the Italian style, with terraces that bore many nymphaea and grottoes.

Two years earlier, in 1597, the king had asked his future father-in-law, Francesco, the grand duke of Tuscany, to send him his finest fountain-maker, Tommaso Francini. The gardens at Foutainebleau were constantly being added to, and Francini had already designed a variety of fountains, including the famous Tiber Fountain and Fountain of Diana. But his finest creations were at Saint-Germain-en-Laye, where he built nymphaea containing magic caves inhabited by water-powered automata just as impressive as those the grand duke boasted at Pratolino.

In his *Antiquités et richesses des villes et châteaux*, published in 1602, André du Chesne describes his wonderment at the ingenuity of Francini's creations: "His grottoes are artistically lined with row upon row of oyster and mussel shells . . . a nymph in half-relief, beautiful and graceful with a laughing face, her fingers powered by the water, playing the organ."[21]

In addition to this, the Grotte de la Demoiselle, there are three others, dedicated to Orpheus, Perseus, and Vulcan, respectively. All were full of spectacle: Perseus smiting a sea monster with his sword, Tritons blowing conch shells, and a dragon spraying water from his mouth and moving his head and wings.

Like those built by Palissy, Francini's grottoes have not survived the passage of time. But many of the engravings of Abraham Bosse show them in all their richness of ornamentation. In 1615 the French engineer Salomon de Caus described how they worked in his *La Raison des forces mouvantes*, where he illustrated the various mechanisms of these automata in minute detail, as well as suggesting some of his own moving fountains. The mythological world of the lost paradise they invoked, mingling the sacred and the profane, was a foretaste of the English gardens of a century later. As a Huguenot, Salomon de Caus was forced to flee

Tommaso Francini
*Orpheus's Grotto in the Gardens of the Château Neuf
at Saint-Germain-en-Laye*
After an engraving by Abraham Bosse, 1559

France, and he went to work at the English court before eventually gaining employment with the margrave of Heidelberg.

We have an idea of what these grottoes looked like because some of them have been perfectly preserved. At Wideville, near Paris, the nymphaeum built in 1630 by Louis XIII's superintendent of finances, Claude de Bullion, is a delightful example of these grottoes, where the landowner and his guests would assemble at "the hour of the nymphs," or bath time. Their purpose was not to bathe—bathing pavilions had not appeared in gardens since the Middle Ages—but simply to gain spiritual refreshment from the sight of the water reflecting the silvery mother-of-pearl surfaces of the mussel shells and the pink interiors of the conches, as well as the brilliance of the amethysts and polished pebbles that ornamented the grotto. At its center, a mask recalls the figures made by Giuseppe Arcimboldo. The nymphaeum is very much an evocation of Italy, even though the artists and craftsmen who made it were French: Simon Vouet, who painted the frescoes; Jacques Sarrazin, who created the stucco designs; François Marchant, who designed the ironwork; and Jacques le Jeune, a pupil of Francini, who produced the hydraulic system. The decoration of nymphaea and grottoes was not the only attraction in the gardens of Wideville. Some of the nymphs appeared distinctly malicious and caused the visitor who gained entrance to their dwelling considerable surprise.

In Italy the grotto had been an essential feature of garden design for more than a century. Likewise, fountain making had become an art in its own right. But not all owners were able to afford automata in their grottoes; automata were usually built only by the wealthiest nobles. So the less affluent sought something else, and this was the beginning of the use of humor in the garden, which was so popular in the Italian gardens of the seventeenth century, though the more serious idea of the garden as a path toward initiation was not forgotten.

A number of artists were summoned to courts abroad to create tricks and jokes based around fountains and water, which had become increasingly fashionable around the beginning of the seventeenth century. In 1613 Archbishop Marcus Sitticus invited the architect Santino Solari and the sculptors Hieronimo Presto and Bernardino Zanini to design gardens for his residence at Hellbrunn, near Salzburg, and furnish them with a number of these highly ingenious trick fountains.

In Italy, too, the owners of the great villas on the hillsides of Frascati were busy placing jets of water in the nymphaea in their gardens. The jets were activated only when a person passed by. Charles de Brosses recalled a "very damp" day he spent in the gardens of the Villa Aldobrandini in 1739. At Collodi, Count Garzoni asked his architect Diodati to create a "trap" in the Neptune's Grotto he had built on the first terrace of his gardens, using concealed fountains.

Near Lucca, at Camigliano, Marquis Nicola Santini did the same. Not only did he conceal the fountains inside his beautiful nymphaeum, but he did so with all the fountains in the little *giardino segreto* in front of the nymphaeum. As soon as the visitor trod on the first steps leading into the garden, the fountains unexpectedly sprayed him. The lower level was occupied by dark arcades containing malicious-looking marble nymphs. The marquis's guests, by now somewhat wet, passed along the central avenue and entered the grotto beneath a curtain of water. Once inside, they might be excused for thinking they were protected from the water and could safely admire the black and pink lava decoration that emphasized the whiteness of the sculptures in the niches. But they hoped in vain. More water spouted through the oculus in the center of the grotto, under the amused gaze of the wind gods and grimacing masks, which, in their turn, sprinkled the visitor with water.

These malicious grottoes were less successful in France. Cardinal Richelieu was really the only person to enjoy soaking the guests who entered the grottoes in the gardens he relaid in the Italian style in 1630: "Visitors were obliged to leave their swords at the door because of the disorder that sometimes arose when someone became angry at the soaking they received."[22]

Louis XIV asked André Le Nôtre to design a similar grotto near the château at Versailles shortly after work began, but in 1674 Charles Perrault changed it into a Palace of Thetis, containing Apollo and his horses, a mythical setting for the plays the king liked to put on in his gardens.[23] In general, the French court was too much aware of the age of chivalry and propriety to want to indulge in such playful games, preferring instead to dazzle the visitor rather than amuse the owner at others' expense. But this did not mark the final disappearance of nymphs from the gardens of France. During the eighteenth century their popularity returned, when Italy once again became a source of artistic inspiration.

The horses of the sun (detail of the grotto at Versailles)
André Félibien, *Description de la Grotte de Versailles*, 1679

Disquieting shadows

The Temple of True Friendship lies
Beside the entrance doors divine
Of goddess Astraea's sacred shrine,
Where cruel love has bidden me
To serve it for eternity;
As hitherto it ruled my days,
It now demands I give likewise
My nights so full
Of tragic sighs.

Honoré d'Urfé, *L'Astrée*, 1610

3
Château de la Bastie d'Urfé, Forez
Rebuilt by Claude d'Urfé, c. 1555
ABOVE AND OPPOSITE, ABOVE: Salle de fraîcheur
decorated with terminal figures of nymphs and fauns
OPPOSITE, BELOW: Courtyard of the château

1

Château de la Bastie d'Urfé, Forez
Rebuilt by Claude d'Urfé, c. 1555
Salle de fraîcheur
ABOVE: Bas-relief figure of Claude d'Urfé
OPPOSITE, ABOVE, RIGHT, AND BELOW: Triton
OPPOSITE, ABOVE, LEFT: Head of a faun

2

3

4

1

Château de Wideville, Seine et Oise
Ironwork by François Marchant
Stucco by Jacques Sarrazin
Frescoes by Simon Vouet
Fountains by Jacques Le Jeune
ABOVE AND OPPOSITE, BELOW: Nymphaeum, 1635–40

The attraction of coolness

2

The Bath of the Nymphs
at Wideville

3

LEFT AND OPPOSITE, BELOW: The Bath of the Nymphs
Francesco Colonna, *Dream of Poliphilus*, 1546

4

1

Château de Wideville, Seine et Oise
Nymphaeum, 1635–40
LEFT, ABOVE, AND OPPOSITE, BELOW: Rock, crystal,
and shell decorations

OPPOSITE, ABOVE, RIGHT: Masks of shells and
rock work
André Félibien, *Description de la Grotte de
Versailles*, Paris, 1679

Veitshöchheim, Bavaria
Gardens of the residence of the Bishop-Prince of
Wurzburg, 1763–91
OPPOSITE, ABOVE, LEFT: Dragon in the Grotto of the
Belvedere, 1772–73
Stucco by Materno Bossi

2

Mysterious evocations

3

4

5

In the Garden of Flora of the Villa Torrigiani

Camigliano, Lucca
Villa Santini-Torrigiani
Garden of Flora, secret garden built by
Count Nicola Santini, late seventeenth century
ABOVE: Entrance to the Nymphaeum
RIGHT: Wind god
OPPOSITE: Jupiter

Comic images of the elements

In the Garden of Flora of the Villa Torrigiani

3

Diverting the eye by means of perspective,

4

The gardens of Versailles, 1662–87, André Le Nôtre
The Grand Canal, 1668–79

1

Chantilly, Oise
The Grand Staircase, 1683
Daniel Gitard
BELOW: Front view
ABOVE: Detail

2

3

Captivating the onlooker with the combination of sea and sky,

Vaux-le-Vicomte, Seine et Marne
ABOVE: The grottoes, front view
OPPOSITE, ABOVE, RIGHT: Allegorical figure of the
Tiber by Lespagnandelle

4

1

Bedazzling through the effects of light and shade,

The gardens of Versailles, 1662–87
ABOVE: Basin of Apollo
Apollo on His Chariot, 1668–71
Jean-Baptiste Tuby
RIGHT: Northern flower bed, 1665–66
Venus Ashamed, 1696
Bronze based on a marble by
Antoine Coysevox, 1684–86
OPPOSITE: Water flower bed, 1683–85
The Rhône
Jean-Baptiste Tuby

2

Of all your light I am the source;
The brightest stars that run their course
Around the sphere surrounding me,
For their brilliance depend
Upon the splendor that I lend.
And from the chariot bearing me
All men desiring me I see,
For Nature's realms are in my power;
The world its only hope doth glean
From the radiance of my beams.

Molière, *Les Amans magnifiques*, 1670

3

1

The gardens of Versailles
ABOVE: Dragon Basin and Allée d'Eau, or Allée des Marmousets, 1663–80
Based on an idea by Claude Perrault
OPPOSITE: *Cupids Fighting the Pythian Dragon*, 1666–67
Gaspard and Balthazar Marsy

And deafening the ear with the wild music of a waterborne battle.

3

2

4

Whether at Sceaux, Chantilly, or Versailles, the dazzling effect created by avenues bathed in sunlight and tumbling cascades of water could not exist without the presence of the woodland growing along either side of the design's central axis. These little areas of greenery, clearly delimited by paths crisscrossing through them, were an important feature of Le Nôtre's work, for they added to the picturesque nature of his gardens.

At Versailles again, Le Nôtre used his artist's awareness of the importance of light and shade in the Allée Royale, the central avenue dedicated to Apollo. The Sun King himself produced a guide to show his guests around the garden, which he called *La Manière de montrer le Jardin de Versailles*. A visit guided by Louis would begin to the left of the main central axis at the Parterre du Midi. After descending the Cent Marches, the visitor would pass by the orangery by Jules Hardouin-Mansart. In front of this was a veritable carpet of "gold and green, which go so well together,"[17] as Mademoiselle de Scudéry declared in her enthusiastic manner. Groves created for recreation, open-air balls, and festivals were planted. From the labyrinth, where thirty-nine painted lead statues of animals illustrated *Aesop's Fables,* the king's guests would come to the Salle de Rocailles, or Salle de Bal. Here they could admire the water cascading down past gilded lead lamp holders and vases onto steps of *rocaille* and shells brought back by the French navy from the Red Sea and the Indian Ocean.

The walk continued through the Bosquet de l'Ile Royale and two huge areas of water linked by a walkway, its design reminiscent of a flower bed. The decoration focused on a series of delightful sprays of water from fountain basins bordering the smaller of the two areas of water, as though the whole scene were suddenly being illuminated. It was here, before the area was completed, that the third day of the "Plaisirs de l'Ile enchantée" took place, a three-day festival held in May 1604.

The colonnade was the last grove where the visitor would stop before the end of the morning's walk. The bright light was filtered by the leaves and played on the reflections of white and pink marble and the violet or turquoise interludes in the transparent architecture of Jules Hardouin-Mansart. The pastel light of the

sky, the transparency of the architecture, and the water's reflective qualities all combined to create a nostalgic vision of antiquity, further reinforced by Girardon's sculpture of Pluto and Proserpine.

In the afternoon, the visitor would be conducted around the various groves to the right of the Allée Royale, where the variety of effects created by the water, and the light filtering diagonally through the hedgerows, created scenes that were both refreshing and beautiful: "The cascades of water, rushing water, water under pressure, foaming, white water . . . calm water reflecting changes in the light or the opaque blackness of shaded avenues, all this complex of dynamics is a triumph by Le Nôtre."[18] But this was a short-lived triumph, for the many groves of trees took on a more classical form and function after the gardens were redesigned by Mansart at the beginning of the eighteenth century.

When the king showed guests around his gardens, the subtle interplay of sprays of water released in unexpected ways in the Bosquet de l'Encelade, the Bosquet de l'Obélisque, the Bosquet des Trois Fontaines, and the Water Mountain and Water Theater created a varied, mutable landscape where the visitor experienced one surprise after another. Eventually, he would walk up the Allée des Marmousets, designed by Claude Perrault, to the Parterrer du Nord and the palace itself. The last scene in the garden is Girardon's *Bain de Nymphes* and *Pyramide d'Eau,* before Apollo himself provided the great finale in the form of a sunset.

There was still more splendor to come after nightfall, when festivities would be organized by the king's master of entertainments, Jean Berain, against the magnificent background of the gardens. "Thus, the whole park served both day and night as the scenery for an endless, enchanting theater. The operas of Quinault

Sceaux, Paris
Aurora Pavilion, 1670
Claude Perrault
Aurora leaving Cephala to illuminate the universe
Ceiling by Charles Le Brun, 1672

and Lulli were written specially to be performed here, and the silhouettes of the garden's groves were the backdrop to the plays of Molière."[19]

Versailles was the site of many of the most spectacular entertainments provided by the king, although he preferred to spend the summer months there and the court was not properly installed there until 1682. The "Plaisirs de l'Ile Enchantée" of 1664 were held to inaugurate the work that had just begun on the gardens and took place in front of the groves of trees. The première of *Princesse Elide* by Molière was presented here, and four years later, in July 1668, Versailles was the enchanting setting for the *Grand Divertissement Royal.* Lulli and Molière wrote the comedy-ballet *Georges Dandin* especially for the occasion, and this was played beneath a pergola covered with beautiful tapestries and lit by thirty-two crystal chandeliers, creating a scene so bright that it was like daylight.

The least expected of the celebrations took place on the Grand Canal in August 1674. Here, "we suddenly saw all the flower beds encircled with lights. In the middle of the fountain basins and these lights, we saw a thousand jets of water, which appeared like roaring silver flames giving off a multitude of sparks. When their Majesties had gazed upon the beauty of these illuminations," continued Félibien, describing the festivities that took place in July at the king's behest, "they boarded richly decorated gondolas, followed behind by the court, also traveling in beautifully ornamented vessels." And he adds, "Then we saw the water in the canal, calm and unruffled, but seemingly swelling with pride at being privileged to bear the most great and august the world has to offer."[20]

The historian can only reply in the lines of La Fontaine: "All parks were once gardens in our ancestors' time, all gardens have turned into parks: the knowledge of the masters changes simple townspeople's gardens into royal ones, just as the gardens of kings are changed into Gardens of the Gods."[21]

1

The gardens of Versailles
Fountains of the Four Seasons
Designed by Charles Le Brun, 1672–75
ABOVE: Basin of Flora
Jean-Baptiste Tuby
RIGHT: Basin of Saturn
François Girardon
OPPOSITE: Basin of Bacchus
Gaspard and Balthazar Marsy

2

The rhythm of the seasons and the woods . . .

Dances and celebrates in the Salle des Rocailles . . .

1

2

4

3

5

The gardens of Versailles
Bosquet du Labyrinthe, 1666–67
Designed by Charles Perrault, built by André Le Nôtre
Fountains illustrating *Aesop's Fables*
OPPOSITE, ABOVE: The Swan and the Crane
ABOVE, LEFT: The Kite and the Birds
LEFT: The Battle of the Animals
Charles Perrault, *Le Labyrinthe de Versailles*, 1677

Bosquet des Rocailles, or Bosquet de Bal, 1680–85
André Le Nôtre
ABOVE, RIGHT AND OPPOSITE, BELOW: Urns by Louis Le Comte
and Etienne Le Hongre, torchères by Pierre Mazeline and Pierre Le Gros

1

And strolls beneath the Colonnade.

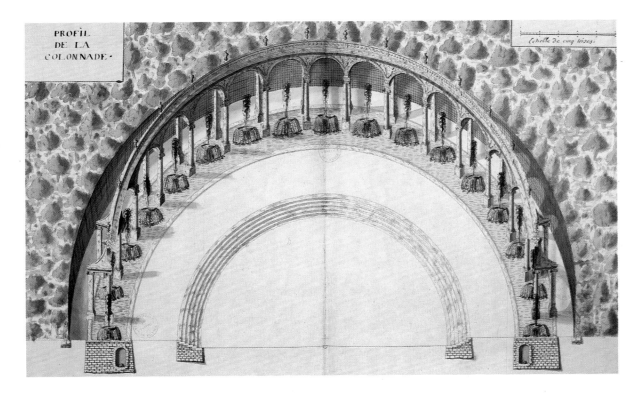

André Le Nôtre
View of the Colonnade
India ink and watercolor, c. 1685

2

84

The gardens of Versailles
ABOVE AND OPPOSITE, ABOVE: The Colonnade, 1684
Jules Hardouin-Mansart

3

1

Comedy in the Bosquet des Dômes,

2

The gardens of Versailles

Bosquet des Dômes, formerly
Bosquet de la Renommée, 1684
ABOVE AND RIGHT: *Acis and Galatea*, 1667
Jean-Baptiste Tuby
BELOW: *Nymph*, 1704
Anselme Flamen

OPPOSITE: Bosquet de l'Encelade, 1675–77
Gaspard Marsy

3

There she is, inhuman; round her Zephyrus sighs,
Her lily roselike hue attracts his eyes.
Young, foolish god, seek thou another rose,
And let her alabaster breast repose.
In vain you court this charming damsel here;
'Tis I alone her beauty may revere:
A fickle lover he would always be,
But what gain I for all my constancy?

Jean de La Fontaine, *Galatée*, c. 1680

4

$\mathcal{T}$ragedy in the Bosquet de l'Encelade.

The courts of Europe are entranced by French design,

Weikersheim, Baden-Württemberg
Gardens of the castle
Original design by Daniel Matthieu, 1708
Redesigned with orangery by Johann Christian Lüttich, 1719–23

1

Schwetzingen, Baden-Württemberg
Gardens of the residence of the
Elector Palatine, 1753–80
Nicolas de Pigage, architect
J.-L. Petri, master gardener
French Garden, 1753
ABOVE: Fountain of Arion
Barthélemy Guibal
LEFT: Avenue of the Lions

2

And captivated by Italian scenography.

2

3

Château de Schönbrunn, Vienna
Built for Maria-Theresa of Austria, 1743–49
Nikolaus von Pacassi, architect
Ferdinand von Hohenberg, master gardener
ABOVE AND LEFT: Fountain of Neptune

OPPOSITE: Belvedere Palace, Vienna
Festal Pavilion, built for Prince Eugene of Savoy, 1723
Johann-Lukas von Hildebrandt, architect
Dominique Girard, master gardener
South facade

1

Caserta, Naples
Gardens of the royal residence, 1752–80
The Grand Cascade
Luigi and Carlo Vanvitelli
ABOVE: Basin of Ceres
LEFT: Basin of Diana and Actaeon
OPPOSITE: Overview of the Grand Cascade

2

Sublime extravagance at the royal residence of Caserta

THE LIBERTARIAN ITINERARY

France, Italy, and Germany in the Eighteenth Century

Veitshöchheim, Bavaria
Gardens of the residence of the Bishop-Prince of
Wurzburg, 1763–91
Johann Prokop Mayer
Summerhouse, 1771–73

etween the time of the great chivalric festivals and the time when the tricolor appeared on the battlefield bearing the words *La liberté ou la mort,* the history of the eighteenth century can be regarded as a backdrop against which the impetus toward freedom first fused, then ignited, and finally flickered to a tragic close."[1]

Before the reign of Louis XIV was over, the society around the throne was beginning to discover this new freedom for itself. Few were absolutely ready for it, and for nearly fifty years not only was the king in complete command of all ceremonies and entertainments, but it was he who ordained every minute of the day, every step of the itinerary through his gardens at Versailles or Marly, and every detail of his courtiers' lives.

But in 1712 the deaths of the dauphin, his wife, and one of their sons had obscured the once-dazzling splendor of the court. The new austerity meant that members of the nobility were suddenly on their own and had to find ways to occupy their leisure hours, which were no longer governed by the king. This new emptiness in the lives of the aristocracy had to be filled. No longer were they being asked to fight at the head of one of the most illustrious armies in the world; no longer did they represent all that was glorious about their country. They had now become "a class of landowners who had been uprooted,"[2] and they no longer took any interest in their lands other than to sell them to the middle classes, who were gradually coming into their own.

The nobility recognized the existence of these rich merchants, manufacturers, and financiers, but only for their money. Not only were they unaware of the people who surrounded them and ministered to their needs, but they often failed even to see them. There was nothing unusual, for example, in a countess appearing naked before her valet as he filled her bath with hot water or put some more wood on the grate, for as far as she was concerned he did not exist.

So when Louis XIV died, the aristocracy found itself alone again, back in the real world. Even at the court, the ceremonials that took place during the Regency period were hollow and empty, "taking place only because convention demanded it, no longer a splendid manifestation of absolute power."[3] Not only did the government lose all its substance, but the state's coffers were as empty as the great deserted halls of the royal residences and their gardens, which were no longer being maintained with such munificence. In 1698, 100,000 *livres* were spent on the gardens at Marly; in 1712, only 5,000.[4]

Courtiers and gentlemen, freed from the shackles of the court, began to organize their own pleasures to stave off boredom, the affliction they feared most. Playing the libertine was the only course they could take, and it was their first "experience of freedom."[5] This emancipation of the senses, "impatient with anything that restrained it, drunk with idleness and easy pleasures,"[6] was reflected in the basic, primal sensations that thinkers and philosophers were beginning to advocate. At the beginning of the century, John Locke had shown how "we are constantly urged to flee the life of emptiness, and to pursue through ephemeral sensations and thoughts a fullness and intensity which requires constant renewal."[7] If we prefer the existence of the senses to that of reflection, and the sensual instead of the rational, constantly seeking new sources of emotion, we inevitably adopt a different view of nature.

The great royal residences, even though they were no longer flourishing and no longer tended by armies of gardeners, allowed guests and visitors to experience the novelty of densely overgrown avenues. Louis XV gradually had the hedgerows at Versailles replaced with leafy trees. The groves became more secret and hidden and the gods and goddesses they contained less distant when they were covered in moss. The subtle sensations one experienced—the coolness and shade and the perfume of the flowers—like the sensations people pretended they experienced through libertinage, required a new garden design. These new gardens, situated not around royal residences but around smaller pavilions, hermitages, and country retreats, were designed for small-scale ceremony rather than large-scale spectacle. But they were also governed by new sets of rules: fantasy, variety, allowing

forward or back without it really mattering. A century earlier, Mademoiselle de Scudéry had already laid down the rules of this game of *galanterie,* the essential prelude to the fulfillment of desire. She showed in her *Carte du Tendre* of a century before how the libertine followed a path with no preordained route, but one in which nature was full of artifice. Visitors could make their way between the *Village de la Nouvelle Amitié* and the *Rives de la Mer Dangereuse* before setting off for Cythera.

This was like the society games where "the use of masks, disguises, and nonexistent obstacles keep one in a constant state of delighted anticipation."[15] The game could be played out among gardens and groves of trees, designed by artists to submit nature to the pleasurable whims of man, with carefully cut hedges, avenues planted with neat rows of trees, and mazes, whose attractions were starting to be rediscovered. All of these elements encouraged games of tag or hide-and-seek, where the aim is to "slip around without being seen, spy on others, and to be discovered in one's hiding place."[16]

Designs for urns for exterior use
Jacques-François Blondel, *De la distribution des maisons de plaisance*, 1737

During the Regency, courtiers, nobles, and the rich upper classes (whose lifestyle often exceeded that of the aristocracy) ordered new mansions and country houses in ever-increasing numbers. For their gardens, they naturally asked their architects for the kind of libertarian scenes depicted on the ceilings, pillars, and paneling of their drawing rooms and boudoirs. The king himself began to dislike the kind of spectacle his residences at Versailles and Marly represented. He merely ensured that these parks were kept in reasonable order, and where anything was visibly falling into disrepair, such as the Basin of Neptune at Versailles or the Grand Cascade at Marly, now overgrown with grass, he had it restored or refurbished. But he gained little satisfaction from his gardens, for they did not reflect his own tastes. They did not give him the savage pleasures of the hunt like the forests of Fontainebleau, or the delights of the opera, although he planned to build one of the finest opera houses at Versailles. But above all, these huge open spaces offered none of the intimacy of his mistresses' apartments or the pavilion in the Parc aux Cerfs, which was described as "a huge harem in the Oriental style, a garden of mysterious woodlands, enchanted pavilions, and a swarm of does of varying degrees of timidity pursued by a libidinous monarch."[17]

More officially, Louis XV satisfied his preference for more intimate places, where his doings would be kept quiet rather than trumpeted to the world, by redesigning the land to the west of the Château de Trianon, which Jules Hardouin-Mansart had built for Louis XIV. In 1750 his architect, Jacques-Ange Gabriel, placed in the middle of the garden he had designed a small octagonal pavilion, which later became known as the Pavillon Français. The king wanted to offer this Salon de Compagnie et de Jeux, as it was then called, together with the surrounding gardens, to Madame de Pompadour as a setting for her little frivolities.

The four identical sides of the building open onto four avenues, giving a choice of four different winding routes leading to a variety of groves. The curves of the decorations and the paths that link them are in contrast to the strict straightness of the main avenues. Here the architect created a unity between the pavilion and

CHIVALRIC GARDENS FOR THE FRENCH COURT

the garden that reflected the duality of the pursuit of *galanterie:* the dual symmetry of the architecture and the strict organization of the flower beds, which masked the elegance of the building and woodlands and yet offered tantalizing glimpses of both. The garden represented "grace without affectation, the dignity of order and the promise of intimacy."[18] The secret charm of the garden was to change when the architect built the Petit Trianon along the axis of the pavilion. But before this occurred, the enchantment of the garden was reinforced by a trellised pavilion, the Salon Frais, at the end of one of the paths, not fully hidden but nevertheless ideal for dalliance away from prying eyes.

Louis XV was not the only person to appreciate these constructions, which allowed light to enter but prevented those outside from seeing in. According to Blondel, these fragile edifices were also found in the gardens of many of the nobility, for "this style of architecture was neglected for many years because people realized that it was expensive and impermanent, but for some time now they have returned to fashion, for the pleasure they provide exceeds their cost."[19]

One of the members of the nobility who succumbed to the attractions of the trellised pavilion was Louis-Joseph de Condé. He had a number of groves designed to beautify the walk across the huge gardens of his property at Chantilly. The prince used these flimsy edifices to decorate the gardens, where games of skill, games of chance, and games of love were played in turn.

His guests would first be shown the enclosed garden of the Pavilion of Sylvia, newly decorated with porticoes and trellised arbors, giving even more charm to the place, which was already full of memories for lovers of *galanterie.* This small pavilion had originally been built by Henry IV, a friend of the owner, who was also besotted with his daughter, Charlotte. Later on, Marie Félicie Orsini, the wife of Henry II of Montmorency, used it to shelter Théophile Viau in his flight from parliament. As a mark of his appreciation, the poet dedicated the finest of his poems to her, calling her Sylvia.

After the garden, the image of the *Village de la Nouvelle Amitié* in Mademoiselle de Scudéry's book, the prince's guests would be led on to more frivolous pleasures. A life-size *jeu d'oie* board awaited them, "played in a newly created grove, with stones marking the numbers of the squares and the geese themselves mounted on pedestals."[20] Further on, to complete their amusements, there was an alley used for the game of pall-mall and a small replica of the maze at Versailles. Once these games had been exhausted, the games of *galanterie* could begin on the Ile d'Amour. Here, refreshments would be served in the Pavilion of Venus, which consisted of three trellised rooms.

Among the king's entourage, another person who succumbed to the pleasure of these new gardens with their graceful geometry was Madame de Pompadour. She had them laid out around all the country houses, hermitages, and châteaux that she ceaselessly bought and sold. During almost twenty years of her "reign" at court, she lived in fourteen different residences in the area between Versailles, the surroundings of Paris, Fontainebleau, and the Loire.

At Bellevue, between Saint-Cloud and Meudon, the architect and gardener Jean-Charles Garnier l'Isle designed a garden for the small château that Lassurance L'Aîné had just finished building for Madame de Pompadour in 1750. A series of groves created an itinerary designed to revitalize the spirits of her honored guest, the king, who was gradually losing interest in her, though she remained his "favorite" until her death in 1764. After stopping at the Pavillon des Bains to admire *Venus in Her Bath* and *Venus at Her Toilet* by her favorite painter, François Boucher, they continued on to the Bosquet d'Apollon and the Bosquet de l'Amour, where they saw "a statue of Madame the Marquise, executed in marble by Jean-Baptiste Pigalle. In the highest part of this pretty grove, made up of nothing but roses and jasmine, there was a gilded leaden canopy supported by palms."[21] The walk continued to the Bosquet de la Cascade, tiled with white marble, where tritons, naiads, and cherubs riding on the backs of dolphins frolicked in a basin amid sprays and jets of water.

Madame de Pompadour was always in debt, and in 1757 she was forced to sell Bellevue to the king. But moreover, she tended to prefer pageantry and spectacle to the rather quieter pleasures of walking in the garden and playing games in its groves. At her hermitages at Compiègne and Fontainebleau, and more particularly at her homes in Versailles and Paris, she liked to organize theatrical events with operas and ballets specially written by the king's musicians, such as Jean-Joseph Mondonville. And although the marquise de Pompadour ordered her gardeners to accord the utmost care and attention to the flower beds of her *maisons de plaisance,* this was only for their carpets of flowers, especially roses, with their tints as

Trianon Gardens, Versailles, begun 1687
Garden urn

delicate as those she used to decorate her dressing rooms and salons. They were flowers whose freshness lasted forever. Once again, artifice was more attractive than nature.

Madame de Pompadour's brother, the marquis de Marigny, who on his sister's death at the age of forty-two inherited her last acquisition, the Château de Ménars on the Loire, was one of the first to realize that nature can create sensations as well as arouse emotions. In 1770 he commissioned Germain Soufflot to build a temple, the Rotunda, at one end of the terrace. This was designed for his young, somewhat frivolous wife. More important, he designed a "secret garden" at the far end of the property, near the banks of the river. Here an area of water hidden in the shade of the garden's woodlands reflected a small nymphaeum, the Grotte d'Architecture, where the marquis engraved the words *piccola ma garbata* ("small but graceful"). This was a cool refuge from the outside world, but not a shelter for the pursuit of libertarianism. For the aesthete marquis, it recalled a time when nymphs bathed freely and heralded the melancholic reveries that nature was soon to provoke.

During the years of Louis XV's reign in France, the quest for pleasure was the main means of escape from the machinations of melancholy in the courts of Europe. The libertarian landscape also fascinated the aristocracy of Germany and Italy. Abroad, *le goût français* no longer meant the wide open spaces evoking the age of Louis XIV; it was extended to include more intimate patterns of paths.

At Charles Theodore's court in Schwetzingen, as we have seen, Nicolas de Pigage had built a huge garden in the French style. But aside from the revenge the elector wanted to wreak upon the king, who ordered his troops to ravage the Palatinate during the wars of 1689, he wanted to be seen as a modern man. He loved to surround himself with the great minds who gravitated toward the court of Louis XV, or at least to correspond with them. He liked the dual plan submitted by his architect, for it involved completing the semicircular flower bed and the broad avenues stretching out from the building to a design full of unexpected features. Along its winding paths were a Temple of Apollo, built on top of a secret nymphaeum, a bathing pavilion, and the famous "Theater of Birds," all concealed among the trees.

Thirty years after work began, in 1783, the elector followed the latest trend in garden art by adding an enormous English-style park. The "Grand Canal" became a lake with a Chinese bridge, and to the temple, the bathing pavilion, and the "Theater of Birds" were added the buildings that had become so popular: a mosque and some Roman ruins.

A few years earlier, in 1744, Margravine Wilhelmine of Bayreuth, sister of Frederick II of Prussia, designed gardens for her home in Bavaria, which she justly called "Sanspareil." These were inspired by Fénelon's allegorical epic poem, *The Adventures of Telemachus.*[22] They included grottoes, cliffs, caverns, and a sad and severe hermitage, all designed to inspire edifying thoughts, which were not at all in accord with the French-style *galanterie* that was in favor in the courts of Germany. But at "Sanspareil," "all was but artifice and the will to astonish."[23]

Through illusion, the libertine society of the age could discover all the diversions in vogue at the time. A small open-air theater was simply a fake ruin, and the sad hermitage contained a delightful "Hall of Coolness," decorated with shells, where monsters and dolphins greeted the visitor with unexpected sprays of water. In the park, nymphs were shown being carried off by satyrs, and hidden in the woods were pavilions of stone and trelliswork that invited the visitor to repose a while.

Near the margravine's home in Bayreuth, the Bishop-Prince of Wurzburg decided to have the gardens of his summer residence at Veitshöchheim redesigned. His architect, Johann Prokop Mayer, undertook the project from 1763 to 1776, concealing beneath the strict geometry of avenues and groves a highly libertarian garden, where "all is pleasure, all is amusement, all is intimate."[24] He designed the park in three separate moods, with a crescendo of sensations building up until the visitor was inextricably involved in the gardens.

From a huge area of water functioning as a theater, where musicians played around a representation of Mount Parnassus, a large number of avenues branched off, some covered with arbors and others lined with hedges. The hedges were arranged as labyrinths, with the sole purpose of amusing visitors, but carefully sited gaps in the hedges led them to little secret pavilions and green enclosures where the scent of roses filled the air. Everywhere, allegorical figures of nymphs, dancers, and musicians by the sculptor Ferdinand Tietz pointed the way to denser

CHIVALRY IN EUROPEAN COURTS

Veitshöchheim, Bavaria
Gardens of the residence of the Bishop-Prince of
Wurzburg, 1763–91
Mask of a muse on the bust of Calliope
Ferdinand Tietz

groves, where a theater of greenery and exotic pavilions and fountains marked the end of the visit. At the end of one of the avenues, a belvedere stood beside a grotto. Inside the belvedere was a round room and individual enclosures guarded by fantastic animals made from shells and stones emerging from the incrustations.

All the decorations in the parks of the sixteenth century were used to enliven the festivities that took place in them, their effect enhanced even further by the *commedia dell'arte* performances given in the evenings in the grass amphitheaters that graced many of the parks and gardens of the time. Once the Pierrots, Columbines, and Harlequins had finished playing, they would pass on their costumes to the dancers in the masked balls that would follow.

The Italian aristocracy, particularly in the Veneto region, were past masters at the art of moving to a summer residence, and to them an open-air theater was more important than any other feature in the decoration of their gardens.

Near Padua, Count Antonio Capodilista preferred illusion to reality. So passionate a drama enthusiast was he that he had the rooms of his villa at Montecchia (built

Marlia, Lucca
Gardens of the Villa Reale, begun 1651
"Teatro di verdura," c. 1700

in 1570 by a rival of Palladio's, Dario Varotari) painted in *trompe l'oeil* so that they could be used as scenery for the plays that were performed beneath his loggias for his guests. Creating even more confusion among them, he even had one of the rooms painted to resemble a garden so that the guests did not know whether they were indoors or out. An arbor covered in vines opened out on the courtyard of a Venetian palace, where he might even show a different play to a different audience. When the count created this effect, which resembled two mirrors facing each other and thus reflecting the scene an infinite number of times, he deprived his audience of any ability to perceive space as it really was. By the use of artifice, he could create the same dizzying effect as the "libertarian" gardens.

Once the last performances of masques and travesties by Goldoni or Gozzi had been played, drama disappeared from the gardens. The libertarian itinerary was over, but the "hall of mirrors" effect continued inside the pavilions, where other pleasures awaited.

Drawing rooms and boudoirs welcomed the visitor with scenes where "the artists of pleasure created voluptuous images in growing profusion, thus both promoting and illustrating the creed of epicureanism."[25] The paintings on the ceilings and varnished walls merely reflected the balls, concerts, and banquets that followed one another within the rooms, "the ultimate game of appearances, in this magnificent image of a life devoted to the pleasure of appearances."[26] These "follies" were eventually organized around one single pleasure: "Pleasure has its own particular realm: a parallel world, which is both homogeneous and many-faceted, with its own temples provided by the 'follies,' its own opening to the outside world, the 'garden,' and it has its own altars and intimate scenes in the form of the 'boudoir.' "[27]

From the country retreat, where one spent several days at a time, to the little belvedere hidden among the woodlands, these small buildings, often built as a single story, tended to follow the same overall plan. A large entrance hall would open onto a huge central drawing room with rich paneling and a ceiling, often a semicupola, decorated in stucco and *trompe l'oeil*. On either side, placed close together, would be two or three boudoirs or private rooms on a less grand scale. The subdued light and the numerous mirrors combined to give the feeling that one was still in one of the groves in the garden. As the architect Le Camus de Mézières stated in 1780, "everything has its part to play, using the magic of painting and perspective to create illusions."[28]

If the layout of these pavilions was much the same from one to another, they served different functions from one place to another. Throughout the courts of Europe, in Italy, Germany, and France, parks and gardens contained at least one of these little buildings, each serving a clearly defined purpose and given over to whatever happened to be in fashion at the time. Each of them, whether summerhouse, belvedere, exotic pavilion, or pavilion for bathing or games, provided particular pleasures to evoke sensations that needed to be renewed during every waking moment. But all of them obeyed the same conventions ruling the game of seduction.

In Florence, among the entourage of Peter Leopold I, who inherited the grand duchy of Tuscany from his father, Francis of Lorraine, coffee drinking became a favorite pastime, so the pavilions in their gardens became *Kaffeehäuser*. All the nobles and upper classes followed the grand duke's Viennese tastes—he was the son of Maria Theresa of Austria—and had their favorite drink served in their own pavilions. At the top of the Boboli Gardens, the *Kaffeehaus* built by Zanobi and Giuseppe del Rosso for Peter Leopold I allowed him to meet his companions beneath the imitation trelliswork of the great drawing room. The tiled terrace allowed everyone to enjoy the evening coolness of the gardens. Beside the central hall, two small boudoirs, whose doors were concealed in a *trompe l'oeil* wall painting, offered all the intimacy anyone could desire.

The Bavarian court, which was soon to become the main rival to that of Austria, preferred French fashions. The latest, imported to France from the Far East during the previous century, was *chinoiserie,* which invaded the drawing rooms and boudoirs of Bavaria, from its mantelpiece decorations to its crockery and wall hangings. The great sea-trading companies, mainly from England and Holland, brought back ever-increasing quantities of goods from the East to satisfy this new demand: engraved or painted lacquerware, fine porcelain, and braided silk. These objects were naturally expensive, and they were soon being copied by manufacturers in Holland from 1614 on and shortly afterward in France.

Louis XIV himself was highly enthusiastic about this new vogue, and in 1670 he had the Porcelain Trianon built in the gardens at Versailles, near the Grand Canal. This fragile, ephemeral-looking pavilion was the first example of this type of building in a European court, though it was only an imitation of real *chinoiserie* from Holland. The walls were covered in blue-and-white Delft pottery. The interior was decorated with blue motifs "in the fashion of works from China," and the furniture, with "porcelain-style decorations," gave it its Oriental charm.[29] But the pavilion lasted only until 1686, when it fell prey to bad weather.

At the beginning of the eighteenth century, when the elector of Bavaria himself sought the sensations that the riches of the Orient provided, he remembered the pavilion built by Louis XIV, which he would have seen during his exile in France. In 1716 he asked his architect, Joseph J. Effner, who had been staying in Paris and had frequented the studios of Germain Boffrand, to build him a pavilion for his gardens at Nymphenburg that would evoke the Far East in the same way as that at Versailles. But the exoticism of the Pagodenburg, which was completed in 1719, was tempered by the architecture, and particularly the paneling, both of which were very much in the French style. Only the Delft tiles bearing Chinese designs and the lacquered panels allowed Maximilian-Emmanuel to "escape into a different moral universe, in a climate where his wishes can be fulfilled without too much resistance."[30]

Before the Pagodenburg was even completed, the elector began demanding new pleasures, this time of water and the relaxation provided by bathing. In 1718 Effner had built him another pavilion for the purpose, the Badenburg, with a huge Delft swimming pool. Drawing rooms and boudoirs added to the pavilion's pleasures. On the first floor, a small Chinese salon hung with wall fabrics bearing pictures of mandarins recalled the pleasures of the Pagodenburg.

Baths and bathing houses were beginning to find favor with the aristocracy once again, after having been scorned since the late Middle Ages. Architectural treatises were again giving long illustrated descriptions of how to install them, and because it was often difficult to fit one in an existing building, they provided the perfect excuse to build a new pavilion hidden among the woodlands in one's garden.

The habit of taking baths obviously fulfilled the newfound need of hygiene, but above all they were a prelude to other pleasures. The owner of the great Collodi gardens near Florence, Marquis Romano Garzoni, had four musicians playing in a gallery while his guests relaxed in the basins below. The men's and women's baths were separated, but a little discreet dalliance was not out of the question.

The Elector Palatine also had a bathing pavilion built in his gardens at Schwetzingen by Nicolas de Pigage. Beside the pool itself, he placed a number of smaller rooms designed for informal dinners and a study for his more serious guests. Although one of these rooms is an example of the current taste for *chinoiserie,* the pool itself was strongly redolent of Italy, with sumptuous wall hangings and two graceful imitation-marble naiads made by Josef Pozzi.

In the French court, Louis XIV had already set the tone and triggered a new fashion for *maisons de plaisance* ornamenting the parks and gardens of princes. Louis XV continued the trend toward pavilions for festivities and games, offering Madame de Pompadour the delightful little buildings constructed by Gabriel near the Grand Trianon.

Aristocrats and members of the upper classes who had risen to the nobility continued building hermitages and what they called "bagatelles" in and around Paris, but their main purpose was to live a life devoted solely to the pursuit of libertarianism rather than following the trends that were starting to be seen in the courts. "There was a veritable mania for these little houses," says one of the characters in Diderot's satirical story, *Bijoux indiscrets.*[31] And ever since the female roles in ballets and operas had started to be played by men dressed as women, or by castrati, at the end of the previous century, aristocrats had started protecting female dancers and singers and setting them up in these little "follies." "The rich man has a wife, a mistress, a townhouse, and a 'little house.' Although little effort was made to hide these indiscretions, they nevertheless required a place set aside for the purpose, and the actress, who was a virtuoso at the art of dissembling, was the very woman these houses were designed for."[32]

Outside Paris, upper-middle-class industrialists had seen a considerable improvement in their fortunes since Jean-Baptiste Colbert, the controller-general, allowed them their new privileges. Inevitably, they also wanted their own little country retreats that, even if not as extravagant as those of the aristocracy, at least looked similar. As their wealth accumulated, they found it easier to justify living in the same kind of luxury as the nobility.

It was with this very aim of enjoying himself in only slightly less libertarian fashion than the Parisian nobility that one of these *nouveaux riches,* the owner of the Manufactures Royales at Abbeville, north of Paris, built his own pavilion. In 1685 his grandfather, Josse Van Robais, and a number of other Dutch master clothmakers set up the first cloth factory in the area at the request of Colbert, who wanted to cut back on imports from abroad. Because of their royal patronage, the Van Robais family became the most prestigious in the town.

Abraham Van Robais, the grandson of the dynasty's founder, created his *pavillon de bagatelle,* a place where he could greet his clients amid beds of roses and let them sample the pleasures of the cuisine of Picardy. His "folly" is one of the few outside Paris that still retains its original decoration, despite the addition of another story at the end of the century. The painted *boiseries* and delicate bouquets of roses and foxgloves aroused the admiration of the poet Michel-Jean Sedaine, who wrote of it: "This retreat would give pleasure even to the gods. . . . The modern art it contains is so fine that it seems beyond the realms of nature."[33]

It was nature, seen in all its glory in the form of foliage, flowers, and fountains, that was the pretext used for building these pavilions. In an age that constantly sought new types of pleasure, nature, which is in a constant state of change, satisfied these needs.

LEFT: *The Dinner*
ABOVE: *After Dinner*
Engravings after Nicolas Lavrience, c. 1780

*The nymphs of love despoil the fields of their lilies
and roses, make them into garlands and use them to adorn
their golden tresses.*

*They dance and sing with their loved ones in a
little retreat where deep shadow hides the banks of the
river from the sun.*

Pietro Metastasio, *Le Printemps*, 1742

1

𝒩*ature prepares to please . . .*

2

3

Schwetzingen, Baden-Württemberg
Gardens of the residence of the
Elector Palatine, 1753–80
Nicolas de Pigage, architect
Garden of Pan and Galatea
OPPOSITE: Bath of the Doves
ABOVE: Statue of Pan
Simon Peter Lamine

LEFT: *Scrupulous Nymphs*
Engraving after Nicolas Lavrience, c. 1780

1

Schwetzingen, Baden-Württemberg
Gardens of the residence of the Elector Palatine, 1753–80
Nicolas de Pigage, architect
Circular trellis leading to the chivalric garden

2

Beginning under the trellises

and the trellised pavilion . . .

Veitshöchheim, Bavaria
Gardens of the residence of the Bishop-Prince of Wurzburg, 1763–91
The Dancing Marquis, 1767–68
Ferdinand Tietz

Chantilly, Oise
Gardens designed by André Le Nôtre for
Le Grand Condé, 1663–83
LEFT: Pavilion of Sylvia, 1604
Rebuilt 1684; trellises added c. 1753
BELOW: Ile d'Amour and Pavilion of Venus, c. 1760

3

4

A musical diversion, the "Theater of Birds."

3

4

Schwetzingen, Baden-Württemberg
Gardens of the residence of the
Elector Palatine, 1753–80
Bird Theater
Nicolas Pigage
OPPOSITE: Trellised arbors
ABOVE: Basin of the rotunda

LEFT: The aviary at Castellazzo
Marc'Antonio Dal Re, *Delizie della villa di Castellazzo*, 1743

1

Schwetzingen, Baden-Württemberg
Gardens of the residence of the
Elector Palatine, 1753–80
ABOVE: Temple of Apollo, 1764–c. 1776
Nicolas de Pigage

Hidden from prying eyes,

Veitshöchheim, Bavaria
Gardens of the residence of the Bishop-Prince of
Wurzburg, 1763–91
OPPOSITE, ABOVE, RIGHT: Belvedere, 1772–74
J. P. Geigel, architect; Materno Bosso, stuccoes
OPPOSITE, BELOW: Summerhouse
Johann Prokop Mayer

Young Woman Taken by
Surprise in a Garden
Engraving after Nicolas Lavrience, c. 1780

2

3

Summerhouses and belvederes

4

To play with nymphs . . .

A darkening, quiet eventide,
An enigmatic afterglow,
Its half-light doth all lovers hide,
And a pleasant coolness show;
Such languor doth this time inspire,
Such contemplative lethargy,
Where Man can dream of happiness,
And all his idylls clearly see.
And now this troop of idle dreams
Fly around him as they shake
Oblivion's dew from off their wings.

C. A. Demoustier,
Lettres à Emilie sur la mythologie, 1789

The Mysterious Swing
Engraving after Nicolas Lavrience, c. 1780

3
Château de Ménars, Loir et Cher
Gardens of the marquis de Marigny, begun 1764
Jacques Germain Soufflot
OPPOSITE, BELOW: Rotunda or Temple d'Amour, c. 1770
ABOVE: Nymphaeum or Grotte d'Architecture

At nightfall.

1

2

3

4

5

Montecchia, Padua
Villa Capodilista, 1570
Chamber with *trompe-l'oeil* greenery
LEFT AND OPPOSITE, ABOVE: Ceiling, sixteenth century
Dario Varotari
ABOVE AND OPPOSITE, BELOW: Walls, eighteenth century

Nicolas Lancret
Dinner of Ham
Oil, 1735

1

2

Jean-François de Troy
Dinner of Oysters
Oil, 1734

Aschaffenburg, Bavaria
3   Gardens of the archbishop of Mainz, Schönbusch,
1775–95
Banqueting and festival room

4

Nymphenburg, Munich
Residence of the Elector of Bavaria
Badenburg Pavilion, 1718–21
Josef Effner
Reception hall

The pleasures of each pavilion—

Schwetzingen, Baden-Württemberg
Gardens of the residence of the
Elector Palatine, 1753–80
Nicolas Pigage, architect
Bathing Pavilion, 1760–70
LEFT AND OPPOSITE, BELOW: View from the gardens
and the Bird Theater
BELOW AND OPPOSITE, ABOVE: Pavilion draperies
Stucco by Josef Anton Pozzi

1

2

The Bath
Charles Jacques Louis Rochette de La Morlière,
Angola ou Histoire Indienne, 1746

3

4

The preparations for seduction,

5

The dances and festivities,

Trianon Gardens, Versailles, begun 1687
French Pavilion, containing the
reception and games room, 1750
Jacques-Ange Gabriel
Exterior view and sculptural details

Nicolas Lancret
Dance in a Pavilion
Oil, c. 1720

The final hesitations

in "trompe l'oeil" gardens,[1]

Abbeville, Somme
Château de Bagatelle, 1753–54
"Folie" built by Abraham van Robais
OPPOSITE, ABOVE: View of the entrance courtyard
BELOW, RIGHT: The Salon d'Eté
RIGHT AND OPPOSITE, BELOW: Detail of the paneling

3

ABOVE: "Valmont and Emilie," illustration for
Choderlos de Laclos, *Les Liaisons dangereuses*, 1782
Engraving after Nicolas Lavrience

4

5

1

2

Avenue de Paris, Versailles
Formerly Grand and Petit Montreuil
Comtesse de Provence's Music Pavilion, 1781
Jean-François Chalgrin
LEFT: Entrance
ABOVE AND OPPOSITE, ABOVE: *Trompe-l'oeil*
decorations in the Round Room

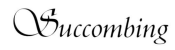

Succombing

*To the heady perfume
of the flowers.*

3

BELOW: Nicolas Lavrience
Scène galante
Sepia wash, c. 1785

4

FIVE

EXOTICISM

*England, France, and
Germany in the
Eighteenth Century*

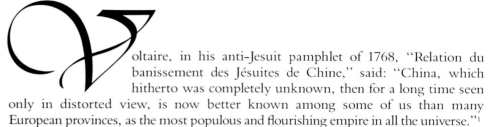oltaire, in his anti-Jesuit pamphlet of 1768, "Relation du banissement des Jésuites de Chine," said: "China, which hitherto was completely unknown, then for a long time seen only in distorted view, is now better known among some of us than many European provinces, as the most populous and flourishing empire in all the universe."[1]

And indeed, for nearly two centuries, Portuguese, Dutch, English, and, finally, French navigators made the Celestial Empire into Europe's main supplier of luxuries. The manufacturers of tableware, silk, and tapestries, first in Holland and then in France and Germany, found a new source of inspiration in China and created their own decorative designs and motifs, which painters and engravers used in their work. Eventually, the preoccupation with *chinoiserie* became almost an obsession.

The particular predilection of artists and architects for Chinese gardens arose mainly from the close relations the Jesuits had maintained with the Chinese for the last two centuries. When the Society of Jesus was founded in 1534, its members were sent to the Far East to continue the work begun by the Dominicans in the thirteenth century. But their first mission was a disaster. In 1552 Francis Xavier, one of the founders of the society, died of malaria on the island of Shangchuan, near Macao, waiting in vain for a merchant to take him to Canton, the main port of the Chinese empire. Despite this tragic loss, Rome continued to send missionaries to the East, where they stayed in Macao itself.

This tiny port, opposite Hong Kong and overlooking the Bay of Canton, was occupied by the Portuguese in 1557 and became their sole point of contact for trade with the Chinese. It was from here that the first Jesuit Father to arrive in Peking left in 1582. When Father Matteo Ricci arrived in China, he received permission from the viceroy of the province of Kwangtung to create a mission in the town of Zhaoqing, about thirty miles from Canton. There he learned Chinese, began wearing the robes of a Chinese scholar, and adopted the name of Li Ma-Teou. In 1595 he left the town, accompanied by a Tartar merchant, and six years later he entered the gates of the Imperial City, nearly three hundred years after the only missionary ever to be received by the Mongol court, Brother Jean de Monte-Corvino.

The presents Father Ricci took with him—chiming clocks, a globe, and even a harpsichord—as well as his erudition, got him through the gates of the Forbidden City, where he was welcomed by the emperor. Soon he was teaching mathematics to the court dignitaries and natural sciences to the Imperial Prince. From then on, the Society of Jesus maintained excellent relations with the court, even when conflicts over Chinese rites begun by the Dominicans in 1710 led to the persecution of all the religious congregations that had been set up in China.

Around the time Father Ricci was being presented to the emperor, other nations besides Portugal—Holland, in particular, with its East India Company, set up in 1602—sent their own ships to reconnoiter the Chinese coast. The company established offices in Ceylon and in 1619 took the island of Java from the Portuguese and founded the port of Batavia, now Jakarta.

Although they had no trouble bartering with Chinese merchants, neither the Portuguese nor the Dutch ever received permission to set up trading posts on the coast. When the governor of Java attempted to send a delegation to the emperor, led by Jan Nieuhof, the request was firmly, though politely, refused:

> The winds are so dangerous on the coast that they could damage your vessels, and their loss would grieve me greatly. I would welcome it if you were to send your ships, though only once every eight years. Then you could unload your goods on the riverbank and into a building specially reserved for you, without having to conduct your dealings on the sea outside Canton. It has pleased me to make this suggestion in your interests and for your own safety.[2]

Despite the failure of this attempt to establish a base in the Celestial Empire, Holland successfully continued trading with Chinese merchants and managed to

Chanteloup, Indre et Loire
Pagoda built for the duke of Choiseul, 1775–78
Nicolas Le Camus de Mézières
View from the lake

set up offices on Formosa, which was less tightly controlled than the port of Canton.

France was also attempting to gain a foothold in Asia. In 1664 Colbert created the French East India Company, but none of its ships ever reached the China Sea. His successor, Michel Le Tellier Louvois, sent six Jesuit mathematicians to the court in Peking in 1685 to work in the Academy of Sciences. Like his predecessors, Emperor K'ang-Hi welcomed the Jesuits enthusiastically, for they allowed him to satisfy his fascination with mathematics, astronomy, and astrology.

After the death of Father Ricci, Father Adam Schall, who had been in China since 1620, was asked to preside over an astronomical tribunal to reform the Chinese calendar. In 1670 Father Ferdinand Verbiest had donated two armillary spheres, one zodiacal and one equatorial, to the new Peking Observatory. A year before his death in 1687, he published the sixteen-volume *Description of the New Observatory*.

When the mission sent by Louvois arrived in Peking in 1688, the emperor immediately demanded that two of its members, Fathers Jean-François Gerbillon and Joachim Bouvet, learn Manchu so that he could talk to them and they could teach him mathematics and geometry. The two Jesuits so gained the king's trust that from 1690 on they went with him on his long journeys through China, often on hunting trips lasting several weeks, and at his request made surveys to be used in a map of the empire. In 1705 eight missionaries were engaged in the task, though the maps were not completed until 1719. Under the title *General Map of the Chinese Empire*, they were first published in Europe in 1737 by the geographer Jean-Baptiste Bourguigon d'Anville in his *Nouvel Atlas de la Chine*.

The emperor actually installed Gerbillon and Bouvet within the perimeter of the palace and lent them a small house surrounded by gardens, which Gerbillon described as "a series of groves of a variety of bamboo, basins, and reservoirs of water, all of them small and decorated with stones of no great richness. This is partly because the Chinese have no idea of what we call buildings or architecture, and partly because the emperor is always at pains to make it known that he will not waste the empire's finances on his own pleasure."[3] This was only the seventeenth century, and the emperor's palace of wood, bricks, and varnished tiles looked very modest to the Jesuits in comparison to Versailles or Marly, which were just being completed.

This missionary was particularly struck by the way the Chinese used stones as a garden ornament:

> Rich people save a little bit of money and spend it on an old piece of rock that has something grotesque and unusual about it, such as being pierced through with a number of holes, as we would on a block of jasper or a fine marble statue. Some of the mountains near Peking are full of beautiful white marble, but they hardly use it except for ornamenting their bridges and tombs.[4]

PRÊTRES ou MOINES DE FÔ,
tirés de Nieuhof.

EAST AND WEST INFLUENCE EACH OTHER

If the Jesuits were fascinated by Chinese tastes, the rest of Europe was well-nigh obsessed. The products that arrived from China—porcelain, lacquer panels, folding screens, and silk goods—were in ever-increasing demand.

In France a new sea-trading company was founded in 1698 to create a regular shipping line to China and break the monopoly enjoyed by the Portuguese, English, and Dutch vessels in the Far East. In March 1699 one of its ships, the *Amphitrite*, left Brest for China. On board was Father Bouvet, who had gone back to France laden with presents for Louis XIV from the emperor. By October the *Amphitrite* was the first French boat to drop anchor in the Bay of Canton. Eventually it made a triumphal return to France, its hold full of precious merchandise it hitherto had had to obtain from Amsterdam or London. Its success led to the creation of the Compagnie Royale de Chine, which flourished until a law was passed in 1716 protecting French manufacturers by forbidding the import of silks and fabrics from the Far East.

In the sixteenth century manufacturers in Holland and France did not think twice about copying Chinese motifs and using them on their own products. We have already seen the success of Delft tiles bearing exotic designs in the court of Louis XIV. Soon the techniques used in the manufacture of the porcelain imported on a large scale by the English and Dutch were no longer secret and were used by the manufacturers of Rouen and Saint-Cloud, and later in Meissen in 1709 and Vienna in 1718.

It was the Germans and Austrians who first thought of arranging their collections of *chinoiserie* in special rooms set aside for the purpose. At Schönbrunn, Emperor Leopold I assembled a collection of screens imported from the Far East, and in 1716 in Pommersfelden, the elector of Mainz, Lothar Franz von Schöborn, asked his cabinetmaker, Ferdinand Plitzner, to make more furniture and woodwork for his "curiosity cabinet," which matched those already in his collection.

As we have seen, the elector of Bavaria was also placing Chinese decorations in his gardens at Nymphenburg at about the same time. At Ansbach, Weikersheim, and Rastatt, the "Chinese Room" was beginning to become as important a feature as the *Spiegelkabinett*, with its walls covered in pieces of broken mirror.

In France, Antoine Watteau became one of the pioneers of this new fashion when he decorated one of the rooms in Louis XV's château at La Muette. Later, in 1725, the Prince de Condé, who had just created the first French porcelain manufacturing company at Chantilly, commissioned a Chinese drawing room for his apartments in his ancestral château. Madame de Pompadour, too, kept up with the fashion of the day by having the walls of her rooms at Bellevue papered with Chinese designs, and she turned the boudoirs off the royal residence at Champs into small exotic drawing rooms.

But the artists of the time were not wholly occupied with commissions from royalty; they were also working for manufacturers. In 1742 François Boucher created a series of designs for the tapestry workshops at Beauvais portraying the Chinese emperor and his court. Along with Etienne Falconet and Christophe Huet, he also produced designs for the Vincennes porcelain factory, which was transferred to Sèvres in 1756.

The decorative engravings of men like Jean Berain and Jacques-Gabriel Huquier soon became famous and played a major part in bringing the designs of the Far East to a wider audience. Until the mid-eighteenth century it was obligatory for any man of quality to decorate his home in the Chinese style.

In Italy the two kings of Naples—Charles VII, residing at Capodimonte, and later Ferdinand IV and his court painter, Nicola Fiore, at Caserta—both fell under the spell of the new fashion. And Gian Domenico Tiepolo proposed to the count of Valmarana that a suite of rooms in his Forestiera at Vicenza be decorated with a variety of scenes, alternating Chinese mandarins and merchants with pastoral scenes and Venetian pageantry.

At the same time, the court of the Emperor K'ien Long, the grandson of K'ang Hi, was itself being invaded by exoticism of a different kind. In 1737 the emperor built himself a number of pavilions along the lines of Versailles, with Italian baroque fountains, in the gardens of his Summer Palace at Yuan Ming Yuan. Brother Giuseppe Castiglione drew up the plans for these "Western follies," consisting of fifteen or so small buildings situated between the various rings of walls. Some of these were openly derivative; the Palace of Delights and Harmony, for example, is a replica of the Porcelain Trianon.

When he arrived in Peking in 1750, Brother Michel Benoist designed a variety of fountains for the gardens, planted with essences imported from France by Father d'Incarville. The emperor and his dignitaries particularly admired the extraordinary water clock at the foot of the stairs of the Palace of the Calm of the Sea. Twelve animals sprayed water into the air in turn for a whole hour leading up to midday, and when the clock struck twelve, all the animals would spray water high into the air in unison. But thirty years later this very fragile mechanism had been destroyed, and the emperor's servants had to form a chain of buckets if they wanted to fill its reservoirs.

Succeeding emperors showed less and less interest in the gardens of the Summer Palace, and in October 1860 they were lost, when English and French troops marched into Peking and burned and pillaged the buildings and razed the gardens. But during the lifetime of emperor K'ien Long, Chinese artists had sketched the gardens for forty engravings used to illustrate a collection entitled *Illustrations and Poems of the Yuan Ming Yuan* (1783), a work that soon became well known in Europe.[5] But it was not these pieces of Western fantasy that most impressed the Jesuits living in Peking. For over a century, missionaries and the rare foreign visitors had been fascinated by the way the Chinese designed their gardens, though some found them too informal.

Europeans, who still had an unbridled appetite for novelty, discovered these gardens after they were described by Jean-Denis Attiret. This Jesuit father had left the Orient in 1738 and had been appointed painter to the emperor when he arrived in Peking a year later. He began writing long letters home, which were published in 1743, about life at the court. In them he described the interior decoration,

DAMES CHINOISES, tirées de du Halde.

OPPOSITE: Priests or Monks from Fo
ABOVE: Chinese women
Jean-François de La Harpe, *Abrégé de l'Histoire
générale des voyages*, 1780–86

architecture, and gardens he had encountered. Some of these were also included in a work entitled *Un récit particulier des jardins de l'Empereur de Chine*.[6]

Although Castiglione's creations were an isolated example of Western design in China, the emperor insisted that the French and Italian artists working for him work in the Oriental style. As Father Attiret recalls: "I had to forget, as it were, all that I had learned and start working in a new manner to conform to the national tastes. Thus I spent three-quarters of my time painting either in oil on glass, or water on silk, trees, fruits, birds, fish of all kinds; rarely human figures."[7]

With the exception of the emperor, who was amused by Western customs, European art and architecture were little appreciated: "They regarded our streets as roads dug between huge mountains, and our houses like rocks stretching to the horizon and full of holes. . . . The idea of placing one story on top of another was particularly repugnant to them."[8]

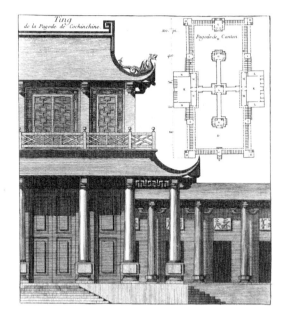

Jean-Denis Attiret was fascinated by the subtlety of the gardens in the Summer Palace, which were still intact when he arrived in Peking. These had been built by Emperor K'ang Hi beginning in 1709. The new imperial residence was situated amid three beautiful parks: the Garden of Luminous Perfection, or Yuan Ming Yuan, where Castiglione built his Western-style pavilions; the Garden of Eternal Spring, or Ch'ang Ch'ouen Yuan; and the Garden of the Mountain of Ten Thousand Years of Longevity, or Wan Cheou Chan.[9]

Attiret saw them at a time when Emperor K'ien Long was continuing to add to the gardens along traditional lines:

> From a small island one can see all the palaces situated at intervals along the edges of the lakes, all the mountains that finish there, all the canals that either bring water to the lakes or have their origin there, all the bridges . . . all the pavilions or triumphal arches that adorn the bridges, all the groves of trees that grow between or in front of the palaces.[10]

Attiret's writings show how extensive the gardens were and that they were laid out irregularly, with no broad avenues but many paths and winding streams: "A kind of beautiful disorder prevails, an antisymmetry."[11] The gardener had sought to create a series of tableaux in which the visitor undergoes a continuous process of discovery, with the stages in his journey marked by benches or pavilions, and each new discovery is accompanied by new emotions. "One enters the garden both as a spectator and an actor in a play. There is both human drama and natural drama."[12] But the garden is designed not to create admiration at the work of man, but that of nature.

In the Lake of the Scent of Snow, the Mountain of Precious Beauty, the Pagoda of the Soft Dew, or the Golden Lake Whence the Springs Flow, the owner of the gardens could enjoy pleasures as intense as they are fleeting. A dignitary might build a pavilion for the sole purpose of being able to watch the moon rise over an almond tree in blossom once a year; another might build a little belvedere to allow him to watch the sun rise and experience the different emotions it produces.

"EXOTIC BAUBLES" IN ENGLAND, FRANCE, AND GERMANY

When the English architect William Chambers, who was working for the Swedish East India Company, arrived in Canton in 1744, and again in 1748, he was fascinated by the search for harmony between man and nature that he could see in any Chinese garden. Once he returned to London, he saw that the painter and landscape gardener William Kent was already following the exhortations of the writers Joseph Addison and Alexander Pope, who were "urging artists no longer to make topiary figures of Adam and Eve, but instead to try to imitate nature."[13] This receptiveness to new sensations that he found among his fellow Englishmen seemed to him to be close to what he had seen in the gardens of China.

When Chambers published his *Designs of Chinese Buildings* in 1757, it turned the idyllic view of nature toward a form of individualism that for a time satisfied an aristocracy constantly in search of all that was new and curious. "The Chinese use nature as their model, and their intent is to imitate it in all its beauiful irregularities,"[14] he declared in a preface to the chapter on gardens. He goes on to list the artifices used to create tableaux, which are different as one goes around each bend in the path, for "the perfection of their gardens lies in the number, the beauty, and the diversity of these scenes."[15] He suggests that a design be adopted where the "marvellous," the "terrifying," and the "peaceful" follow in succession, in accordance with the "drama of nature" found in the gardens of China: "Nothing is more varied than the methods they use to create surprise. They lead you through caverns and gloomy avenues, which you leave to find views of a delightful landscape, enriched with everything which is most beautiful in nature."[16]

Chambers was not able to gain as much knowledge of Chinese gardens as he would have liked, for he was unable to go outside Canton when in China, but in the book he described "a summary of various conversations which he had with a famous Chinese painter named Lepqua."[17] For this reason, many of his English readers found his conclusions debatable. His *Dissertation on Oriental Gardening*, published in 1772, was strongly criticized in intellectual circles, particularly by Horace Walpole and William Mason. Mason produced an ironic parody of Chambers's work in a poem, "Heroic Epistle to Sir William Chambers."

But the artistocracy, particularly those of the court, received Chambers's work enthusiastically. The idea of alternating scenes of enchantment and fearsomeness led first the English and then the French aristocracy to create the new Chinese garden, a kind of theater where the drama of the world was played out. Beside their elegant classical temples, enchanting scenes and exotic pavilions began to appear.

Chambers recommended that "architects take care, like painters, to create these little buildings serving a particular use, or inviting rigour to repose, but attracting one's eye to a scene and allowing it to discover another." He insisted that they exercise a variety in their choice, for "it never fails to please, and novelty which has nothing disagreeable or shocking about it often creates beauty."[18] Gardens and parks were no longer complete without these follies; they were no longer the meeting places of libertarian France as they had been at the beginning of the century, but were now purely decorative.

Chambers was one of the first to build one of these edifices, in 1761. He designed an octagonal pagoda, based on a Chinese one he had seen in Canton, for the Princess of Wales's gardens at Kew. Its ten stories dominate the gardens, which the princess later had her gardener William Aiton turn into botanical gardens, under the guidance of Lord Bute, a famous amateur botanist.

Before this famous pagoda was built, however, two delightful Chinese pavilions had already been created for Frederick II's summer residence at Potsdam in Prussia. The King of Prussia was the only European sovereign apart from Catherine the Great of Russia who still supported the Jesuits, and their missions to China in particular. In 1773, when the three Bourbon monarchs, Louis XIV of France, Charles III of Spain, and his son Ferdinand IV of Naples, asked Pope Clement XIV to ban the Jesuits, the pope wrote to Jean Le Rond d'Alembert: "I am keeping the precious seed so that one day I may give it to anyone who wishes to cultivate this rare plant in his own country."[19]

The king of Prussia particularly admired the erudition of the Jesuit fathers, but when he ordered a pagoda and a teahouse from his architect, G. W. von Knobelsdorff, in 1743, authenticity was not a major criterion. His main aim was to re-create the exoticism of a world whose civilization enchanted him. It was of little importance that these pavilions did not follow the original Chinese designs, which neither he nor his architect was ever likely to see in their natural setting.

In France, after the publication of William Chambers's books, architects were no longer satisfied with such distant relations with Chinese culture. Chambers's *Plan, Elevations, Sections and Perspective Views of the Gardens and Buildings at Kew* had been circulating in Paris after its publication in 1763. His *Designs of Chinese Buildings* had also been widely read in England and Europe even before Louis XV's geographer, Louis Le Rouge, introduced it to France in his *Jardins Anglo-Chinois à la mode* of 1776. By this time almost every aristocrat wanted something of the kind for himself, and strange buildings soon began to be silhouetted against the skyline of the Ile de France: pagodas at Chanteloup, the home of the duke of Choiseul, a pagoda on a bridge of rocks in the gardens of the archbishop of Arras, a Chinese house in the Désert de Retz planned by François Racine de Monville, Chinese pavilions in the gardens of the marquis de Saint-James, the comte d'Artois, the marquis de Marigny, the duke of Uzès, and in the gardens at Cassan and Rambouillet, and even a Chinese dovecote built by the duchess of La Trémoille.

One of the first to follow this new fashion in France was the duke of Choiseul, a minister in Louis XV's government. In 1770 he was exiled by the king to Chanteloup, near Amboise. Far from sinking into despondency, he held court with a group of friends, and the result was so riotous that some complained, including his confidant, the Abbé Barthélemy: "All these people, all this shouting, noise, slamming doors, barking dogs, noisy conversations, voices, waving arms, and gusts of laughter in the billiard room, the drawing room, or the music room."[20]

The duke decided to erect a monument on his land as a gesture of thanks for the faithfulness of his friends. He and his architect, Le Camus de Mézières, chose the pagoda at Kew as their model. Begun in 1775 and finished in 1778, the Chanteloup pagoda was reflected in a huge lake, which the architect created by

OPPOSITE: *Ting* of the Cochin Chinese pagoda
ABOVE: Section of a Chinese house
William Chambers, *Treatise on the Buildings . . . of the Chinese*, 1776

diverting the waters of another lake eight miles away, thus giving it an even more exotic setting.

Above the windows of the ground floor, the duke had engraved the Chinese characters for Recognition, Kindness, Harmony, Brotherhood, and Knowledge. His sentimental reasons for building the pagoda were conveyed by the architect in his design: The pagoda was not a reconstruction of some cheap Oriental bauble but a free adaptation of a model whose form expressed its own essence, without any symbolic connotations. For Le Camus de Mézières it was "the arrangement of forms, both individually and as part of a whole, which become the inexhaustible

The emperor of China's country house
Le Rouge, *Jardins Anglo-Chinois à la mode*,
1776–89

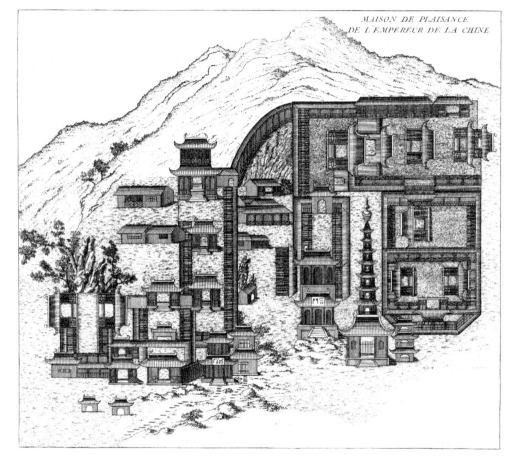

source of illusions. Our attempts to produce impressions with our architecture, and speak to the mind or move the soul, should be based on this principle."[21]

So exoticism was not merely a passing fashion but instead allowed the architect to express transcendental emotions against a background that seemed even more remote than the ancient Greeks and Romans.

Perhaps the pagoda, this token of eternal friendship, was given divine protection for what it symbolized, for today it is the sole remnant of the splendors of Chanteloup. The duke's extravagance bankrupted him, and when he died in 1785, the estates were sold and broken up. The building itself was demolished stone by stone under Napoleon.

One of the last people to take China as a model was Receiver-General of Finances Pierre-Jacques Bergeret. In 1789 he had a magnificent pavilion built on his estate at Cassan. A multicolored octagonal building of wood and glass was built atop a stone mound containing a *salle de fraîcheur*, and the whole construction was surrounded by a broad, sinuous lake. On top of the building, with its curled-up corners, were bronze bells that jangled in the wind. Thus "all the features of Chinese architecture can be seen together at Cassan: water, mineral and vegetable, sound and color. But the pavilion, truly a model of its kind, was still much more an ingenious interpretation than a close imitation of Chinese architecture."[22]

Europeans only skimmed the surface of Far Eastern culture. They never explored it in any real depth, and the manufacturers who used its imagery never made any claim to authenticity. Soon pavilions evoked the enchanted gardens of sultans and maharajas in the same way that pagodas had hinted at the delights of the Chinese empire. And when Louis XV was given some Ottoman tents by the sultan to use as hunting lodges, architects seized on the idea of using them to decorate their patrons' gardens. Louis-François Trouard proposed to the marquis de Marigny that one be placed in his gardens at Ménars, and in Sweden the French architect Louis-Jean Desprez placed two magnificent copper tents with *trompe l'oeil* draperies in the famous gardens of Haga, at the behest of Gustav III.

After the Ottoman Empire, it was India's turn to serve as an inspiration for the last of the princely follies. In 1780, when Charles Theodore ordered Nicolas de Pigage to build a mosque in his gardens at Schwetzingen, his intent was to conjure up not only the mysteries of Islam but an image of the Orient as well. And so the reflection of the mosque in the large water basin in front of it is immediately reminiscent of the Taj Mahal, the mausoleum at Agra, which Shah Jehan built for his favorite wife in 1650.

India was also the inspiration for the future king of England, George IV. In 1818, while still prince regent, he ordered John Nash to redesign the Royal Pavilion at Brighton, basing it on the palaces of the maharajas in Delhi. The art of China already permeated all the rooms of this seaside pavilion: bamboo furniture, porcelain dinner services, wallpaper, chandeliers shaped like waterlilies, and black and gold lacquerwork in the prince's chamber. This royal folly was completed in 1821, the year of George's coronation, as the embodiment of his dreams and a constant reminder of the fairy-tale splendors of his vast colonial empire.

At Brighton, just as at Schwetzingen, the *idea* of using the Orient as a model was more important than the precise form it took, so despite the distance that separated the imitation from the real thing, it lost none of its charm.

Rigobert Bonne
The Chinese Empire
Map published in 1782

François Boucher, "Audience with the Emperor of China"
Sketch for a tapestry, 1742

1

The courts of Europe . . .

2

Antoine Watteau
Chinese and Tartar Figures
Engraving by Jacques-Gabriel Huquier, 1717, after
Watteau's decoration for the Château de La Muette

Leafy enclosure
Jean-François de La Harpe, *Abrégé de l'Histoire
générale des voyages*, 1780–86

3

Under the spell of exoticism:

Vicenza
Villa Valmarana, guest house
Decorations for the Chinese Room, 1757
Gian Domenico Tiepolo
ABOVE: Tribute to the Goddess

OVERLEAF: Mandarins and merchants

"Chinoiseries" fill

drawing rooms and boudoirs

正園花

1

Versailles inspires the architects of the Chinese emperor;

The gardens of Versailles, 1661–87
André Le Nôtre
Allée Royale seen from the
Basin of Apollo

2

3

Gardens of Yuan Ming Yuan, 1737–66
Giuseppe Castiglione, architect
Michel Benoist, fountain design
OPPOSITE, ABOVE: View of the maze
ABOVE: Palace of the Calm of the Sea, east side
BELOW: Palace of the Calm of the Sea and
Water Clock
Copper engravings from drawings by Castiglione,
1783–86

4

Another version

of nature . . .

Désert de Retz, Chambourcy
Estate of Monsieur de Monville,
1774–89
Chinese vase near the
open-air theater

Sommet du Nenuphar.

Sonet du fruit du Nenuphar

Pao tco

Revealed in Chinese engravings

OPPOSITE, ABOVE: Mount Chang Fang and Lake Chou
LEFT: Mountain of Flowers
BELOW: Gardens of the Chinese emperor
Le Rouge, *Jardins Anglo-Chinois à la mode*, 1776–89

3

4

The fragrances of the Far East abound . . .

Botanical gardens, Padua, 1545
Sacred lotus *(Nelumbo nucifera)*

144

Johann-David Schleuen
View of the Chinese Pavilion in the Royal Gardens of Sans-Souci at Potsdam
Tinted engraving, c. 1760

2

At Sans-Souci, in the King of Prussia's gardens . . .

The red Chinese water lily
Buchoz, *Collection Précieuse et*
Enluminée des fleurs . . . , 1776

3

ABOVE: Schwetzingen, Baden-Württemberg
Gardens of the residence of the Elector Palatine, 1753–80
Chinese bridge leading to the English garden, c. 1777

1

2

At Kew, in the gardens of the Princess of Wales . . .

166. pi. Elévation de la Pagode

PLAN
de la
Pagode
Exécutée
à Kew

3

4

Kew Gardens, London
Anglo-Chinese garden, 1757–63
Designed and built by William Chambers for Augusta,
Dowager Princess of Wales
OPPOSITE, BELOW AND ABOVE, RIGHT: The pagoda, 1761–62

ABOVE, LEFT: Plan of the pagoda
Le Rouge, *Jardins Anglo-Chinois à la mode*, 1776–89

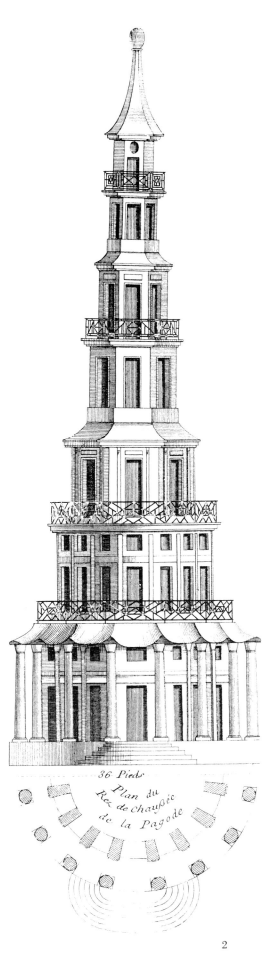

1 Chanteloup, Indre et Loire
Nicolas Le Camus de Mézières
ABOVE, LEFT AND OPPOSITE: Pagoda built for the
duke of Choiseul

ABOVE, RIGHT: Plan of the pagoda
Le Rouge, *Jardins Anglo-Chinois à la mode*, 1776–89

At Chanteloup, on the estate of the duke of Choiseul.

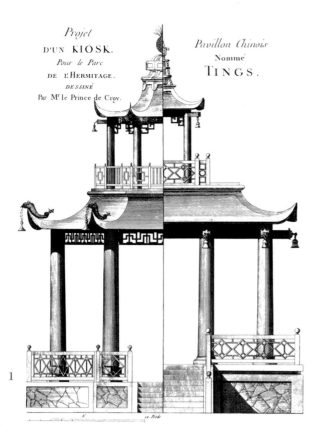

ABOVE: Design for a summerhouse in the hermitage garden, and a Chinese pavilion called a *Ting*
BELOW: View of the summerhouse at Rambouillet
OPPOSITE, ABOVE: The Chinese Pavilion and Philosopher's House at Bonnelles
Le Rouge, *Jardins Anglo-Chinois à la mode*, 1776–89

L'Isle-Adam, Val d'Oise
Cassan gardens of Pierre-Jacques Bergeret,
c. 1788–89
RIGHT AND OPPOSITE, BELOW: The Chinese Pavilion, restored 1971

Chinese "folies" multiply . . .

4

5

TEMPLE MORESQUE

PAVILLON MORESQUE

Pavilion and Moorish Temple
Le Rouge, *Jardins Anglo-Chinois à la mode*, 1776–89

1

2

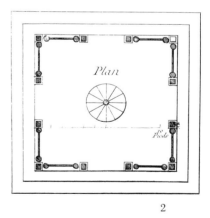

Chiswick House, London
Lord Burlington's villa and gardens
Sphinx

3

4
Veitshöchheim, Bavaria
Gardens of the residence of the Bishop–Prince of Wurzburg, 1763–91
Oriental summerhouse, 1768
Ferdinand Tietz

Exotic baubles are many and varied

1

2

Mirages of the Orient

3

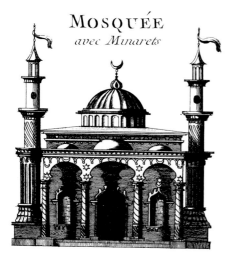

MOSQUÉE
avec Minarets

C

Plan

5   10 Pieds

4

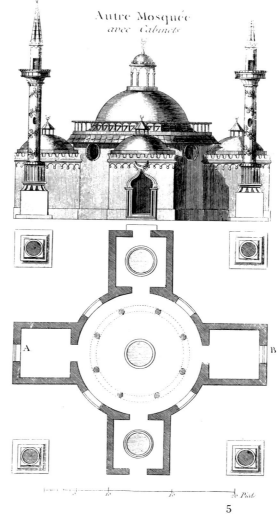

Autre Mosquée
avec Cabinets

A   B

5

Schwetzingen, Baden-Württemberg
Gardens of the residence of the
Elector Palatine, 1753–80
Nicolas de Pigage, architect
ABOVE AND OPPOSITE, ABOVE: Mosque
in the Turkish Garden, 1780

OPPOSITE, BELOW: Louis-Jean Desprez
*Design for the Leather Tent in the Haga
Gardens*
Watercolor, 1787

LEFT: Mosque with minarets and another
mosque with chambers
Le Rouge, *Jardins Anglo-Chinois à la mode*,
1776–89

1

Brighton, East Sussex
ABOVE, BELOW, AND OPPOSITE: Royal Pavilion, 1787
Rebuilt by John Nash in 1818 for the Prince Regent,
later George IV

"We heard a delightful music . . ."
Anonymous, *Les contes des Génies ou les
charmantes leçons d'Horam, fils d'Asmar*, 1766

2

3

The Prince Regent plays at being a maharajah

4

THE ENCHANTING GARDEN

England in the Eighteenth Century

So on he fares, and to the border comes
Of Eden, where delicious Paradise,
Now nearer, Crowns with her enclosure green,
As with a rural mound the champaign head
Of a steep wilderness, whose hairy sides
With thicket overgrown, grotesque and wild,
Access deni'd; and over head up grew
Insuperable highth of loftiest shade.[1]

In these lines, written at the end of the seventeenth century, John Milton evoked the vision of a lost paradise. The Garden of Eden he describes is much like the English countryside, which he once admired so much before he went blind.

The garden is a symbol of an earthly paradise, but it is also a garden flowering with love, a place that is difficult of access, closed to outsiders, like Woman herself. Courtly miniaturists and poets had been painting and writing about it, in all its mystical and sensual forms, ever since the thirteenth century. But by the time garden design became regarded as an art, this image had faded and then totally disappeared.

Pietro de' Crescenzi, one of the first practitioners of this new art, spoke of it in the wider sense of the word: ". . . a method that tends to perfect a natural gift by introducing into it more order, more pleasure, and more usefulness."[2] The garden was no longer the realm of the senses but now became the world of reason. Man began to impose order on what he saw, so the garden became a sign of man's power over his environment and, by extension, the image of power itself.

In its new role, the garden was of necessity dependent on architecture, the art that is furthest removed from reference to the senses. By the sixteenth century the garden had adopted all the main rules of architecture—axiality, symmetry, the correct relationship of the parts to the whole—as well as its imagery, in colonnades, terraces, great flights of stairs, and one of its main ornaments, sculpture.

In seventeenth-century France, the great designs commissioned by Louis XIV all fulfilled the same laws: Function took precedence over form, for everything was built in the service of the prince. Le Nôtre fully accepted these rules, and yet he had already begun to bend some of them. By using water to create large areas of light and flower beds to create areas that were half light, half shade, in contrast to dark patches provided by groves of trees, he was able to stress visual sensations. His techniques were closer to those of painting than of architecture, even though they still involved the deliberate use of perspective.

Le Nôtre's admirers and successors retained only the principles of composition from his many theories about his art (though Le Nôtre himself had not put them fully into practice) and were therefore ill-prepared for the major changes that took place in English gardens in the 1730s.

While work was proceeding apace on the gardens at Versailles, in England the Restoration had enthroned Charles II, a monarch who was full of admiration for the work done for Louis XIV. He sent his own gardener, John Rose, to Versailles to learn how to lay out gardens in the style of the French, and this tradition was continued by his brother, James II, who came to the throne in 1685.

Four years later the king, who had been judged to be excessively Catholic and too friendly with the French court, was forced to abdicate in favor of his daughter Mary, the wife of William of Orange. William came from Holland, a country where flowers were a major industry, and he gave further impetus to the fashion for sweeping perspectives of straight lines with straight-edged flower beds.

William and Mary employed the master gardener William Bentik, who was Dutch by birth. He imposed his personal preference, and that of the court, for highly geometric compartments fringed with high hedges and made extensive use of the art of topiary, which he took to extravagant extremes. Gardens were no longer decorated with hedges shaped like balls or cones but, instead, with a whole

Stourhead, Wiltshire
Henry Hoare's gardens, begun 1741
Temple of Apollo, designed by Henry Hoare,
c. 1765

range of birds, domestic animals, dragons, fauns, and nymphs. There was not a tree, hedge, bush, or square of lawn that escaped the gardener's shears. Groves of deciduous trees were banished to the outer edges of the garden to avoid disturbing the orderly continuity of the design.

Throughout William III's reign, aristocrats close to the court went to George London for their new garden designs. London had left the post of royal gardener, working under William Bentik, and went into partnership with Henry Wise. They had established a sound reputation by the time they were commissioned to design the gardens of the royal palace at Kensington. For twenty years they planted many of Britain's great gardens and helped other gardeners bring the art of topiary to elaborate new heights.

England was reluctant to adopt fashions imposed on it by foreign countries. The court, unlike that of Louis XIV, did not contain the major part of the country's nobility. Many of them preferred to remain country squires, spending their lives at home to look after their lands, so they remained oblivious to the doings of London aristocrats.

Even before the end of the century, in 1685, the diplomat Sir William Temple had criticized English gardens in his book, *Upon the Gardens of Epicurus*. He felt nature was being deprived of liberty and the gardens were stilted and artificial. Instead, Temple wanted to see gardens that brought to life the description of Epicurus's garden, in which "the sweetness of the air, the smell of flowers and the greenness of plants . . . were a perfect aid both to calm reflection and health, quickening the senses and the imagination and giving both body and mind a sweet and agreeable repose."[3]

A few years later, the essayist and editor of *The Spectator*, Joseph Addison, retrieved *Paradise Lost* from the obscurity to which it had been consigned since its publication in 1667. At the time, it had been regarded simply as an expression of regret by a man who was disappointed by the new political order after the restoration of the monarchy.

Joseph Addison was a great admirer of this forgotten poet. To him the garden should be a reflection of Eden as Milton described it—the English countryside:

> *Southward through* Eden *went a River large,*
> . . . .
>
> *Water'd the Garden; thence united fell*
> . . . .
>
> *And now divided into four main Streams,*
> *Runs diverse, wand'ring many a famous Realm*
> *And Country whereof here needs no account,*
> . . . .
>
> *Ran Nectar, visiting each plant, and fed*
> *Flow'rs worthy of Paradise which not nice Art*
> *In beds and curious Knots, but Nature boon . . .*[4]

The regular, symmetrical designs that Milton had rejected were increasingly regarded as the symbol of everything that was restrictive and inimical to freedom at a time when basic liberties were starting to be recognized. Before he acceded to the throne, the king had had to ratify a Bill of Rights, which guaranteed parliamentary authority, freedom of speech, and freedom of elections.

When Anne, James II's second daughter, succeeded William III in 1702, her strict Anglican nationalism was not in any way seen as grounds for criticism: quite the contrary. As soon as she came to the throne, she made sure that her gardens were stripped of everything that could be considered an import from the Continent, such as overelaborate flower beds and complicated hedge designs.

The new attitudes toward gardening techniques that surfaced in the early eighteenth century were merely a reflection of a new attitude toward the function of the garden itself. First and foremost, it lay in a whole new conception of the world of nature and its relationship with art. No longer was art the process of perfecting nature's gifts, for nature was already perfect, or at least it had been before man branded it with his own particular mark; now it was merely a "model." Nature contained the greatness and power that had exalted man and made England the most powerful of all nations. And thus it should be allowed to remain free, like the countryside, unencumbered by gates and fences. The garden became the symbol of this new freedom, this "place privileged with the quest for harmony,

IN SEARCH OF A LOST PARADISE

Cliveden House, Buckinghamshire
Gardens designed by Charles Bridgeman for Lord Ockney, c. 1720–30
Topiary

such that in man the creative power of his nature coincides with the strictest exercise of reason, such that fullness and apparent disorder of nature, with all her whims and mysteries, coincide with human invention."[5]

Like painting, the art of gardening underwent far-reaching change as a result of this new attitude toward nature. As it was a source and origin for some of the most fruitful emotions, nature could no longer be fitted into a system or codified to comply with the criteria of ideal beauty laid down by man. Writers and poets constantly criticized the idea of the formal garden, where this process of denaturing took place in contradiction to the process of artistic creativity. But Addison saw a necessary link between art and nature and attempted to harmonize the two so that both tended toward the same ultimate perfection. He described the importance of this link in a series of essays published in 1712, *Pleasures of the Imagination.*[6] This intellectual pleasure stimulated creativity through the perception of all that was great, extraordinary, and beautiful in nature. The sight of a horizon stretching to infinity liberated the mind of man and excited his imagination; the harmony inherent in a landscape taught him where he could find beauty, and the variety of guises in which nature appears aroused the artist's creative powers.

Addison sought total harmony between art and nature:

> Although the scenes nature offers us are generally more diverting than any artistic representation, the more the works of one resemble those of the other, the more pleasant we find them; because our pleasure comes from a dual principle, that is, from the very beauty of objects which strike the eye and their resemblance to others; we take pleasure in finding a common beauty between them as well as seeing them separately. We can view them either as copies or as originals.[7]

Thus nature is beautiful because it inspires art, and art is beautiful because it is inspired by nature. This close relationship between the two led Addison, after he had defined the pleasures of the imagination derived from landscapes, to seek vicarious pleasures from the memory of things he had seen previously.[8]

Hampton Court Palace, London
Charles II's gardens, c. 1670
Detail of wrought-iron gates by Jean Tijou

EUROPE LOOKS TOWARD ITALY

This need to exalt the power of memory meant that the world of the ancients assumed a new importance, whether described by poets like Homer, Virgil, and Pliny, or seen in the remains of the glory they left behind.

The Grand Tour, obligatory for any English gentleman of the time, was particularly important, for it allowed him to see firsthand some of the great relics of antiquity. But equally important, he could also see the villas and palaces of Rome, Tivoli, and Frascati, which members of the Church and the nobility had transformed into gardens of pleasure in the sixteenth century. By now, the beginning of the eighteenth century, these buildings and their gardens were no longer being looked after with the care and attention their original owners might have hoped for.[9] Because many of them were semiabandoned and nature was gradually covering over the signs of man's genius, they were no longer a source of melancholy for painters and architects. On the contrary, between the power of nature, with its newly liberated forces, and the spectator, interposed as though in the foreground of a picture arising from the past greatness of the place, came the vision of an even more ancient world. It is from here that Addison's vicarious pleasures were evoked.

Thus it was essential to pay closer attention to those who in their writings, their analysis of antiquity, and their own practical work paved the way for a new interpretation of the world. It was they who could help re-create this lost world in all its harmony, this Paradise Regained, despite the enormous distance in space and time. It was in this spirit that Richard Boyle, the earl of Burlington, left London in 1719 in search of Andrea Palladio. He had already seen drawings of Palladio's work, as well as those by Scamozzi, which Inigo Jones had brought back more than a century earlier.

The publication in 1715 of the first volume of architect Colin Campbell's book, *Vitruvius Britannicus,* had convinced Boyle that Palladio was superior to any other architect of his time. In 1716 Boyle had his gardens at Chiswick redesigned to include a number of small Palladian-style temples. The year 1715 also saw the republication of the first part of the *Quattro Libri dell 'Architectura di Andrea Palladio* by Italian architect Giacomo Leoni, who was living in England at the time.[10]

In Italy, Lord Burlington was able not only to see writings and buildings by Palladio firsthand, but he was also lucky enough to find several drawings by him in the stables of the Villa Maser. These he brought back to England at the end of 1719. He was accompanied on his return by a young coach painter who had been training under the painter Bernardo Luti in Rome since 1711. Lord Burlington took a liking to the cheerful and likable William Kent and installed him in

Burlington House, where he stayed until his benefactor's death. He was introduced to many of the popular young architects of London, including Henry Flitcroft, Isaac Ware, and Stephen Wright.

During this period, English garden design was starting to change, although imperceptibly. But theorists and master gardeners could not ignore Addison's writings, and Alexander Pope, who had been preparing a translation of the *Odyssey* since 1715 (eventually published in 1726), had also strongly criticized the subjugation of nature in the name of art. In an attempt to achieve a closer harmony with the spirit of the ancients—particularly Virgil and Homer—he gave his gardens at Twickenham the Arcadian charms of the gardens of Alcinoüs, the father of Nausicaa in the *Odyssey*. The gardens alongside the Thames were planted with weeping willows, and a few years later a temple was concealed behind a grove of trees. A small grotto near the river with its walls lined with shells and glass became a symbol of the inspiration afforded by nature, for the inside of the grotto reflected the scenes outside, with all their infinite variety from day to day and from season to season.

At the same time, the garden designer and author Stephen Switzer, apprenticed to the company of London and Wise, was also contesting established ideas in his book *The Nobleman's, Gentleman's and Gardener's Recreation,* better known as *Ichnographia Rustica* after its second edition in 1718. Recommending that people not lose sight of a garden as "a judicious mixture of the pleasures and profits that the countryside has to offer,"[11] he also began putting the new theories on the relationship between art and nature into practice in his work as a gardener.

But his contemporary Charles Bridgeman, also trained by London and Wise, was the first to put them into practice. In 1709 he began work as a designer for the architect John Vanbrugh, who was well connected in court circles. Vanbrugh was in the process of completing Blenheim Palace, the residence given by Queen Anne to John Churchill, duke of Marlborough, as a gesture of thanks for his victory at Blenheim. Charles Bridgeman was particularly struck by the techniques used by Vanbrugh—who himself had served in the army for more than thirty years—to create boundaries around his buildings. Even his purely utilitarian gardens were surrounded by high walls, which were more reminiscent of military engineering than garden design.[12]

This was a time when people were once again beginning to discover the beauties of the open countryside, and Vanbrugh's approach was destined to be short-lived. Charles Bridgeman's first commission was for the gardens at Claremont belonging to Thomas Pelham Holles, duke of Newcastle, who served two terms as prime minister. His innovative approach was described by Stephen Switzer as "a simple and unaffected manner of enclosing the gardens such that the adjacent countryside looks as though it forms part of the garden."[13] Around the edges of the estate he dug wide, empty ditches and paved the bottoms with stones or bricks. Named "ha-ha's" because of the surprise they provoke when found, they prevent animals from straying onto the lawns of the property but do not obstruct the view in any way.

This new vision of a garden that was no longer self-enclosed but appeared to extend infinitely into the surrounding countryside gave the owner a new importance, for now both he and his visitors could appreciate his heritage. The nobles and gentlemen of England seized on Bridgeman's ideas with enthusiasm, and he was kept busy fulfilling their commissions. But in many ways he was still very much a product of the architectural tradition of garden design—he produced the drawings for his gardens but rarely supervised the actual work—and continued to adapt the classical style that the poets and writers were yet having difficulty making understood. Fountains, flower beds, lawns, and groves were now being placed alongside less formal features, such as open fields bordered with hedges of trees.

Before George II made him successor to Wise as supervisor of his gardens in 1728, Bridgeman drew up plans for many famous gardens, including Rousham in 1721, and Stowe, where he worked between 1725 and 1728.

Stowe was the home of Sir Richard Temple, Lord Cobham, in Buckinghamshire. John Vanbrugh was in the process of enlarging the house and was succeeded in turn by Giacomo Leoni, James Gibbs, and Richard Adam. In the gardens, Bridgeman built a series of basins and cascades leading down to a long canal, which in turn opened onto a huge area of water dominating the whole landscape. After 1770 nothing remained of the gardens, which were closer to the tastes of the French or Italian princes than to those of the English nobility. Later the king commissioned Bridgeman to design gardens for all his main estates—at Windsor, Kensington, Richmond, and Hyde Park.

WILLIAM KENT AND THE ENCHANTMENT OF NATURE

Even before Bridgeman's death in 1738, tastes had changed. The work of this master gardener was almost totally eclipsed by the enthusiastic reception given to the work of Lord Burlington's young protégé, William Kent, who, in the words of Horace Walpole, "broke with the idea of enclosure and saw that the whole of Nature is a garden."[14]

Thanks to his training as a decorator in Italy, to the advice he received from Lord Burlington, and, above all, to the complete freedom he felt in approaching an art that was new to him (he had had no training as a gardener), William Kent attempted to redefine the relationship between art and nature. First, he made possible something that poets and writers had been demanding since the turn of the century—turning the estates of prosperous Englishmen into "a Nature without sin,"[15] where they could pursue the art practiced by the Roman patricians; harmoniously combining *otium* and *negotium,* pleasure and activity.

William Kent's first project as a garden designer was at Chiswick, where the gardens were full of classical allusion created by Lord Burlington, who was himself an architect. The young artist had helped with the interior decoration of his patron's new villa. Work began in 1726 and was finished three years later, the design recalling both Palladio's Rotonda and Vicenzo Scamozzi's Rocca Pisana. In 1727 Kent designed the great exedra where the villa opens out onto the gardens. Here he alluded to the ancient gardens of the Villa Adriana, which he saw during his stay in Rome. This broad esplanade was extended by paths radiating outward, possibly designed by Charles Bridgeman.

In the same year, 1730, William Kent was introduced to Lord Cobham, who had been impressed by the *luogo di delizia* that Chiswick had become and wanted Kent to work for him at Stowe. Here Kent remodeled the east wing of the building, but he left alone the great open esplanade in front of the house. Now that he was on his own and no longer influenced by his patron, the young artist designed a garden that for the first time was seen from the point of view of a painter rather than an architect. A stream winds gradually downward from the top of the gardens into a valley, which became known as the Elysian Fields. The gentle slopes of the fields with their surrounding trees contain two temples designed by Kent himself: the Temple of Ancient Virtue, based on the Sibyl's Temple at Tivoli, and the Temple of British Worthies, completed in 1735, in which the great figures of British history are depicted, including, naturally enough, John Milton. Slightly further away, the Temple of Modern Virtue was built. The exiled Lord Cobham had the temple deliberately constructed in ruins to illustrate a satire on the government by Alexander Pope.

This process of "liberating" gardens—they were freed because they imitated nature and were therefore subjugated to it—was precisely what the owners of the gardens were seeking. Their purpose was to exalt man's noblest feelings before he was corrupted by the artifices of life as a member of society. The owner thus ensured that the visitor found something to reflect upon at every turn of the path. Throughout the work at Stowe, which was not completed until 1790, Kent ordered his architects to build monuments and memorial temples.

These buildings were no longer simply decorations in an Italianate landscape like the Temple of Venus and the Hermitage, which Kent placed at the southern end of the estate in 1732; instead, they were symbols of the high points of English history, or even symbols of the nation itself. They gave the route through the garden a moral value that could easily have concealed their aesthetic importance. It was in this spirit that James Gibbs, who succeeded John Vanbrugh after Vanbrugh's death, built the Temple of Friendship in 1739 and the Temple of Liberty, or Gothic Temple, which showed the will of the English to seek the foundations of their culture in their own gardens.

Even before work was finished at Stowe, poets were starting to realize the evocative power it possessed. Samuel Boyse, in his poem "The Triumph of Nature," described how, in these gardens, nature triumphed over art and virtue triumphed over corruption. Since virtue is borne of disorder, the great variety of scenes created by Kent in his Elysian Fields could only be controlled by a superior harmony: "Here you see order in variety, for all things are different and yet are in harmony."[16] William Gilpin also stressed the harmony created by Kent and Gibbs between the variety of visual effects, which stimulate sensations and the imagination on the one hand, and temples and rotundas, which render human thought fertile on the other: "And if one says that in some parts the gardens tend too much towards the love of the unbridled, the sensual, on the other hand it cannot be denied that they give very noble encouragements to Honour and Virtue."[17]

The Arcadian landscapes at Stowe were not solely intended for those who

LEFT: "Hell," Book II
ABOVE: "Paradise," Book VIII
John Milton, *Paradise Lost*, 1727

wanted to savor the delights of living in the countryside; they were also a reminder of the glory that was England and an attempt to perpetuate that glory. This perhaps is one of the reasons why Palladio's architecture was so popular among the great landowners of the period: They identified with the noblemen of the sixteenth-century Veneto, who gave as much effort to beautifying their gardens as they did to making Venice the greatest seafaring power in the world. Many nobles built a Palladian bridge in their gardens as a reference to the greatness of that city. Palladio never actually built a bridge of this kind, though he reproduced the design for one in his book. It was thus a work of pure imagination, untainted by any contact with practical reality. This small piece of brickwork topped by a portico was frequently used to adorn a river, a pond, or the end of a lake, and it became part of the English countryside, enriching its architectural heritage.

As early as 1717, John Vanbrugh had designed a bridge for Blenheim Palace, but it was never completed in the form he had planned and was not covered over. In 1736 Lord Pembroke designed one for his home at Wilton House, aided by his architect, Roger Morris. At Stowe, the field that slopes gently down from the Gothic Temple was the perfect location for a Palladian bridge. John Wood added one to Prior Park, near Bath, home of the entrepreneur Ralph Allen. Situated at the bottom of the valley that stretches out from the house, its purpose was more decorative than symbolic.

Kent's novel design for the Elysian Fields at Stowe began to increase his renown, and in 1737 James Dormer asked him to remodel the gardens at Rousham, which had been left to him by his elder brother, Colonel Robert Dormer. The initial design was by Charles Bridgeman, but their educated young owner thought the gardens were too strictly conventional and did nothing to evoke nature as Virgil described it.

William Kent followed the same process as he had at Stowe. He did not work to any preconceived design but simply surveyed the land and used his painter's eye to produce a series of india-ink sketches of the areas he found most attractive. He redesigned the gardens to harmonize with the countryside stretching into the distance. Because of the sloping land, the surrounding fields, villages, and woods seem to form part of the gardens themselves. But his main intention was to make the gardens conform to the picture he had of them, and alongside his sketches he placed pictures by painters such as Nicolas Poussin, Gaspard Dughet (Poussin's son-in-law), Claude Lorrain, and Salvatore Rosa, all painters he had come to appreciate through his acquaintance with Lord Burlington.[18] He had loved these paintings on first sight, for they recalled happy memories of the Roman countryside and the hills of Tivoli. The architectural references at Chiswick were transplanted to Stowe with even more intensity, for they could not be produced simply by adding a few architectural features; they involved the whole countryside.

At Rousham, the layout of the gardens takes advantage of the different levels of land, and the visitor encounters a series of views as he progresses along a winding path. Each of these gradually mingles with the next. First, there is a small, delightful valley, the Vale of Venus, which opens onto an area of green with a little temple at one end. In the middle ground, hills bearing ancient groves of trees surround a simple rustic stone hermitage. Below, a river flows along the edges of the estate with a little bridge at one end, and then the visitor's gaze continues uninterrupted into the surrounding countryside. On the horizon, one other feature reminds us that the scene before our eyes is one first fashioned by the hand of nature and full of nature's beauty. An eye-catcher is placed in the middle of a field, at the point where the land and the sky meet. At Rousham this takes the form of a medieval arch a mile away from the house; at Stowe there is a Roman gate, and at Blenheim, among fields full of grazing sheep, there is a memorial column.

After Rousham, Horace Walpole was able to write in *On Modern Gardening* that "William Kent is enough of a painter to feel the charm of a landscape, hardy and firm enough in his opinions to lay down precepts about it, and born with sufficient genius to see a whole built up from our imperfect strivings."[19]

Once gardens had been freed from the rules of architecture, garden designers had to find other artifices to imitate nature. So they took up painting, itself an art of illusion. "All the art of gardens," as Pope said, "must come from the landscape painter."[20] So linear perspective was replaced by aerial perspective, in which the interplay of color in the various areas of the garden was used to suggest depth and create infinite distances that merged imperceptibly with the sky. Great subtleties in contrast were achieved between the dark brown of the foliage, the bright green of the lawns, and the deep blue of the water in rivers, lakes, and ponds.

In William Kent's new design, water served a dual purpose. First, it was the "point of light" described by Horace Walpole, suddenly illuminating a particular part of the landscape and creating constant variety for the visitor. Second, it linked the different points where the visitor stopped to admire the view, and thus created the harmony of a work of art.

This dual function of water—creating unity and diversity at the same time—gave rise to one of the most perfect gardens of the first half of the eighteenth century. In 1740 Philip Southcote and Charles Hamilton had created picturelike compositions for their gardens at Woburn Farm and Painshill. But it was the gardens at Stourhead, on the edge of Salisbury Plain, that reproduced the theories William Kent had implemented at Rousham with more coherence, surpassing even

Attributed to Salvator Rosa
Temple of the Sibyl at Tivoli (detail)
Etching, c. 1740

the gardens on which they were modeled. These gardens in Wiltshire were part of land acquired by the banker Henry Hoare in 1717. In 1741, after a long stay in Italy, his son, Henry Hoare II, took on the job of turning the land into pleasure grounds, assisted by a friend of Kent's, the architect Henry Flitcroft. He worked with the gardens of Rome in mind, where the pastoral scenes he saw brought the poems of Virgil to his lips. When he returned to England, he had even bought a copy by Andrea Locatelli of Claude Lorrain's *View of Delphi with Procession* because it reminded him so strongly of the *Aeneid*. He hoped to re-create the pleasure he derived from these scenes by rooting them in the present, using architectural references, yet distancing the spectator by creating an atmosphere of remoteness.

Between the gently sloping hills was a lake with meandering banks. The subtle arrangement of groups of trees separated the green lawns and served as a backdrop to temples based on Claude Lorrain's work: a Temple of Flora, a pantheon, and a Temple of Apollo. If the visitor followed the intended route through the gardens, none of these landmarks would be a sudden discovery; they were visible from the other side of the lake and were reflected in it, but always at a different angle. These effects of aerial perspective create a veil over the landscape and give the impression Henry Hoare intended—that of coming close to an inaccessible world. Henry Hoare would allow nothing that would alter in any way this jealously guarded idea of a lost paradise, where reality came close to unreality.

The poetic vision of this pleasure garden not only preserves the secret of the eternal beauty of a work of art but also conceals in the depths of an enchanted grotto a statue of a sleeping nymph, sculpted by John Cheere and symbolizing the source of the gardens' inspiration. On the basin where she reclines are inscribed lines by Alexander Pope:

> Nymph of the grot, these sacred springs I keep,
> And to the murmur of these waters sleep;
> Ah! spare my slumbers, gently tread the cave.
> And drink in silence, or in silence lave![21]

In 1780 Henry Hoare II's grandson, Sir Richard Colt Hoare, diminished the charm of the place by constructing a gravel path along the edge of the lake. But at the same time he planted a large quantity of the exotic plants and rhododendrons that were becoming popular among the landowners of the time, who were fascinated both by botany and exoticism.

In 1752 the Jesuit Attiret's description of the gardens of the Chinese emperor K'ien Long, combined with the evocative images of Chinese gardens brought back from Canton by William Chambers, created an even greater infatuation among London society with its passion for novelty. As we have seen, the court was particularly attracted by these picturesque designs, recalling and reinforcing emotions already experienced. Augusta, Princess of Wales, to whom William Chambers had been introduced by her counsellor, Lord Bute, immediately appreciated the young man's talents and asked him to design her new gardens at Kew. Chambers had brought back a good deal of detailed information on Chinese architecture, and he was also in close touch with the new archaeological discoveries that were being made at Rome and near Naples. In 1751, during a long stay in Italy, he visited Herculaneum, which had been discovered only thirty years before.

Bomarzo, Viterbo
Sacred Wood, Château Orsini, 1552–84
Temple

THE TWILIGHT OF ENCHANTMENT

At Kew, Chambers included a number of decorative buildings: a classical temple, a Moslem mosque, a Roman ruin, a Chinese house, and even a reconstruction of the gardens of the Alhambra, as well as the famous Pagoda. The Pagoda is now the only remnant of a garden whose designer gave full rein to his imagination, creating a garden that ennobled the thoughts of all who saw it.

But Chambers was little appreciated by the great landowners of the time. The detachment he effected toward the idea of the edifying image that every garden should represent was not popular. Only the critic Henry Kames, in his essay "Elements of Criticism," quoted his descriptions of Chinese landscapes, for they provoked a genuine aesthetic emotion through the power they exercised over the imagination.

The exoticism of Kew was only an intermediary stage in the art of the garden, and for connoisseurs gardens could only be approached through pictorial art. "Listen then, docile disciple, to my songs, learn how much your art has to learn from painting; painting is a sister art of gardening, learn its rules,"[22] advises William Mason in his poem "The English Garden," written in 1772.

While poets sought the reflection of art by contemplating the mirror of nature, landscape gardeners were pushing the relationship between nature and art to the limits of the possible by removing from their gardens all traces of man's genius, such as summerhouses, temples, and follies. Thus, in the second half of the eighteenth century, the perception of the garden moved not in the direction of Chambers's exoticism but toward the great creations of one of Chambers's rivals, Lancelot Brown. Although there appears to be perfect continuity between their creations, their major difference in intentions led to the loss of the idea of gardens as enchantment.

Lancelot Brown became master gardener at Stowe in 1741, and the ten years he had spent as an apprentice to William Kent had taught him to transcend the simple art of gardening. In 1751 he left his job and set up his own business as a landscape gardener in Hammersmith. Since William Kent had died two years before, he soon began to receive some major commissions from the friends and acquaintances of Lord Cobham. He immediately created "a little ideal universe, perfectly adapted to the society he was working for. The hand of man was no longer visible: instead, Nature was dominant, settled, opulent, well proportioned and feminine."[23]

In all his landscaped gardens, Lancelot Brown accorded major importance to the visitor's perception of the general view of the estate by linking the natural viewpoints. The major feature that provided this link was, of course, water. At Syon Park, built in 1767, a winding stream flowed through the gardens. Since the land was perfectly flat, Brown varied the views by carefully arranging plants and woodland in harmony with the stream. He placed low clumps of irises and waterlilies side by side with larger groups of rhubarb or tulip trees, whose large leaves overlapped the smaller plants; in the background, beeches and oaks completed the composition. When he worked on Luton Hoo, the home of the Princess of Wales's close friend, the earl of Bute, he made a stream a major feature of the gardens, on a scale comparable to that of Blenheim Palace. But at Blenheim, Brown had used a lake instead of a stream when, in 1770, he completely rebuilt Vanbrugh's and Bridgeman's original design.

At Stowe, Brown gave the gardens a new dimension by adding a lake. He replaced Bridgeman's design with a grassy area leading down to the little lake with its octagon, its shores lined with groves of trees, in which Kent had placed his first ornamental buildings. From the perspective of the house, a large gap, marked by two little lake pavilions (originally built by Vanbrugh but completely rebuilt in 1764), leads the eye to the distant countryside, while a Corinthian arch on the horizon serves as an eye-catcher.

There was no symbolic or emblematic path to be followed in Lancelot Brown's gardens. His gardens did not follow any preconceived idea or theory, and they had no hidden function other than that of providing pleasure. Brown viewed nature as an endless series of opportunities to make the garden even more pleasant, and as a result he acquired the nickname "Capability" Brown, under which he passed into history.

In his homage to the doyen of English landscape gardeners, Horace Walpole shows the inevitable impasse that Capability Brown reached: "His great and fine genius remains unrivalled. . . . It is doubtless permissible to say that his sense of synthesis and elegance has never been faulted. But—and herein lies his genius—the more beautiful his successes, the more easily forgotten they were; his representations of nature are so true to life that they risk passing unnoticed."[24]

By hiding any traces of the artist's presence, and at least appearing to make nature the vanquisher in its eternal struggle against man, Capability Brown and his successor, Humphrey Repton, managed to deprive it of all the power that had been ascribed to it for centuries. No longer was there any hidden mystery in nature; no longer was nature the guardian of the sources of knowledge or emotion.

The great flowing, transparent designs of Blenheim and Luton Hoo created none of the emotions that Thomas Whately sought in a landscape. Every scene, every viewpoint for the author of *Observations on Modern Gardening,* should create a range of sensations, from simple contemplation to pure spirituality: "A lake whose waters are deep and dark and covered with a dark shadow which they reflect is a place proper to melancholy."[25] But the landowners themselves no longer wanted gardens that might awake unknown sensations and cause discomfort. Instead, they wanted gardens that were boundless, forming a fixed, perfect, and eternal image of the countryside, which they were in the process of transforming.

The intensive cultivation practiced after 1750, when new laws were implemented governing the enclosure of common land by major landowners, was starting to upset the fragile balance between town and countryside. So these great gardens, where enchantment was giving way to illusion, were perhaps linked with, as Michel Le Bris wrote, "the infernal flames of the forges of Coalbrookdale, the slums, prostitution, and crime,"[26] for they could be seen as an attempt to paper over the cracks in British society.

Cliveden House, Buckinghamshire
Gardens designed by Charles Bridgeman for Lord Ockney, c. 1720–30
Blenheim Pavilion by Giacomo Leoni, c. 1727

Chiswick: a place of delights . . .

1

Vicenza
Villa Almerico–Capra
La Rotunda, 1570
Andrea Palladio

Lonigo, Vicenza
La Rocca Pisana, 1576
Vicenzo Scamozzi

2

John Rocque
Plan of the Garden of the Houses at Chiswick . . .
Engraving, 1736

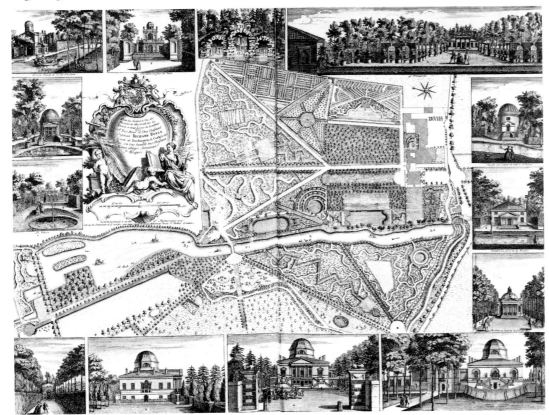

3

Chiswick House, London
Lord Burlington's villa and gardens, 1726–27
Exedra by William Kent, 1727–30

1

Stowe House, Buckinghamshire
Lord Cobham's gardens, 1716–90
Charles Bridgeman, William Kent, and
Capability Brown
ABOVE: Oxford Bridge, 1760–61
RIGHT: Doric arch, 1768
BELOW: Monument to Lord Cobham, 1747–48
James Gibbs

2

3

$\mathcal{S}$towe: the exaltation of noble emotions

Stowe House, Buckinghamshire
The Elysian Fields and the Temple of Ancient Virtue, 1734
William Kent

An architectural game of references:

Palladian bridges
ABOVE: Stowe House, Buckinghamshire, 1742
OPPOSITE, ABOVE, RIGHT: Prior Park, Bath, c. 1755
OPPOSITE, BELOW: Wilton House, Wiltshire, 1736
Designed by Lord Pembroke and built by Roger Morris

172

2

BELOW: "A Stone Bridge
of My Own Invention"
Andrea Palladio,
I Quattro Libri dell'Architettura,
1570

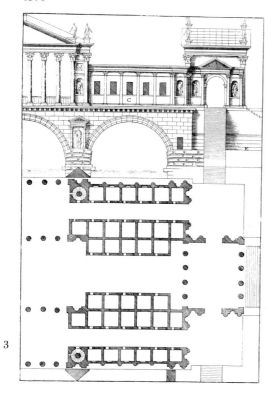

3

The Palladian bridge, symbol of the elite . . .

4

173

ABOVE AND OPPOSITE: Stowe House, Buckinghamshire
Gothic Temple, 1741–44
James Gibbs

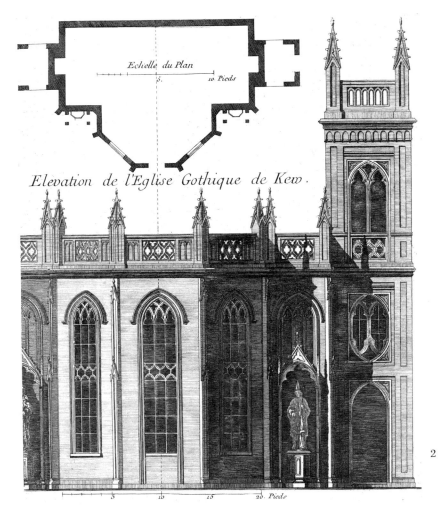

Echelle du Plan
5. 10. Pieds

Elevation de l'Eglise Gothique de Kew.

RIGHT:
Elevation of the Gothic Church at Kew
Le Rouge, *Les Jardins Anglo-Chinois
à la Mode*, 1776–89

5   10   15   20. Pieds

The Gothic temple, symbol of the nation's perpetuity

Rousham: William Kent's idyllic vision . . .

Rousham House, Oxfordshire
Gardens designed for General James Dormer by
William Kent, 1737–41
OPPOSITE, ABOVE: The surrounding countryside with
fake ruins in the background
OPPOSITE, BELOW: Valley of Venus
ABOVE: A fake ruin used as an eye-catcher

Stourhead: a land of enchantment . . .

Stourhead, Wiltshire
Henry Hoare's gardens, begun 1741
LEFT: View of the lake
BELOW: Temple of Apollo, c. 1765
Based on a design by Henry Hoare
OPPOSITE: Pantheon, 1752–56
Henry Flitcroft

1

2

3

The astonished spectator sees with sweet surprise
The sparkling flow of water,
The green lawns appear and the forests rise,
Here, through the dense shade
Buildings pierce their way,
There, the silver lake glides between the banks;
A pleasing diversity enchants the soul,
And the resulting harmony crowns all.

Samuel Boyse, *The Triumph of Nature*, 1742

179

1

Stourhead, Wiltshire
Henry Hoare's gardens, begun 1741
The grotto, 1750–60
Henry Flitcroft
ABOVE, LEFT: View of the lake
BELOW AND OPPOSITE: River god and sleeping nymph
John Cheere

ABOVE, RIGHT: Funerary monument
C.C.L. Hirschfeld, *Théorie de l'Art des jardins*, 1779–85

2

4

Refuge of the nymphs

1

Stowe House, Buckinghamshire
Octagonal Lake and Eleven-Acre Lake, begun 1770
Capability Brown
ABOVE: Grotto
RIGHT: Hermitage by William Kent
OPPOSITE: Corinthian arch eye-catcher, 1767
View along the axis of the manor toward the arch

2

At the lakeside of Stowe,
perfect harmony between art and nature

3

Syon Park, London
Gardens designed for Sir Hugh Smithson, duke of
Northumberland, by Capability Brown, 1767–73
LEFT: Tulip tree
BELOW: View of the river

1

2

Enchantment threatened at Syon Park and Blenheim

Blenheim Palace, Oxfordshire
Gardens designed for John Churchill, duke of
Marlborough, by John Vanbrugh and Henry Wise, begun 1722
Blenheim Lake, 1770
Capability Brown

SEVEN

THE GARDEN
OF
ILLUSION

*France in the Eighteenth
Century*

The gardens of Versailles
Basin of Apollo, 1774–79
Designed by Hubert Robert, built by Thévenin
The Horses of the Sun, 1668–75
Balthazar and Gaspard Marsy

During the fifty years following the Regency period, Parisian society created a large number of follies in and around Paris. These estates, each with a garden of five or six acres, had dramatically changed the somewhat tedious landscape of the Parisian suburbs, which suddenly became a great deal livelier as a result of this renewed activity.[1] By now they were known simply as the Folie Boutin or the Folie Beaujon. The names were descriptive, for they were a perfect reflection of their owners' extravagance. They reached their apotheosis in the most senseless of all follies, built by Louis XVI's brother, the comte d'Artois.

In the early summer of 1777, as a result of a bet of 100,000 *livres* he made with his young sister-in-law, Marie-Antoinette, the count began one of the greatest of all follies. He claimed that in the space of seventy days (the period the queen would be away at Fontainebleau), he could completely rebuild a ruined country house known as "Bagatelle," which he had bought two years before. To celebrate her return, he would give a sumptuous reception.

This "little house," situated at the gates of the Bois de Boulogne near the Château de Madrid, had been the setting for a number of celebrations. In 1720 the maréchale d'Estrées was organizing parties that soon were as renowned as those of his neighbor, Mademoiselle de Charolais, at the Petit-Madrid, or the fine suppers given by the king at the nearby Château de La Muette. Wrote the marquis d'Argenson in 1739:

> At La Muette, where the king is currently staying, the company is happy and independent. They have invited ladies who are used to this company and whom they are used to. We dine *chez Mademoiselle* at the Madrid; we take supper at La Muette, and in the afternoon at Bagatelle we eat with the maréchale d'Estrées; we pass our time very pleasantly, dallying with the women, and everything is very well organized.[2]

Two years after the maréchale died, in 1747, the house changed hands. Its new owner, the marquise de Monconseil, also lead a life of dalliance and party-going. But in 1770, sobered by age and financially ruined by the endless work of restoring a house that had been badly built in the first place and was now falling into decay, she sold Bagatelle to the prince de Chamay. He in turn sold it to the comte d'Artois five years later.

The king's brother intended to win his bet, and as soon as it had been accepted he told his first architect, Joseph-François Bélanger, to draw up plans for a new pavilion to replace the former mansion. The process of compiling the plans and gaining approval for them took forty-eight hours. Eight hundred workers were taken on and work could begin. "Any means may be used to hasten the completion. The mounted constabulary kept curious onlookers at a distance. When more stone, plaster, or other materials were required, they would simply stop a passing wagon destined for someone's private house, seize it, and divert it to where they wanted it."[3] On November 26, 1777, the pavilion was completed and the count won his bet. The building was ready to welcome Marie-Antionette. But the queen claimed to be suffering from a slight indisposition and did not attend the festivities organized to inaugurate the last of the great Parisian follies, which had cost more than twice as much as the count's original estimate.

Bagatelle is the archetypal *petite maison:* a large vestibule on the ground floor, with a billiard hall on its right and a dining room on the left; opposite is the great round-domed drawing room leading in turn to two small boudoirs. The first floor contained more private rooms, bedrooms, and the chief valet's room.

Despite the changes made to the building during the nineteenth century by its owner, Lord Seymour, earl of Hertford, who raised the upper story and built the present dome, Bagatelle is as attractive today as it ever was. Only the paintings that adorned the walls of some of the rooms have disappeared, painted over by the comte d'Artois on religious grounds after he returned from exile in 1815.

Once Bagatelle had been completed, the comte d'Artois took on a Scottish gardener, Thomas Blaikie, to work under Bélanger in the design of the gardens. The two men designed an Anglo-Chinese garden, in keeping with current tastes.

employing an architect or landscape gardener, he asked his "master of ceremonies," Louis Carrogis, known as Carmontelle, to use his skills as a theater designer to create his new gardens. The gardens, in the words of Carmontelle himself, were to be "a pure fantasy, the desire to have an extraordinary garden solely for amusement, and not out of any desire to imitate a nation that makes so-called natural gardens by rolling its lawns and harms Nature by demonstrating everywhere in the garden the art of geometricality so favored by the gardener with no imagination."[12]

As soon as the visitor entered the gates of Monceau, he must have been amazed by the scene Carmontelle had created. Chinese pavilions were followed by a pagoda, its interior lined with painted mirrors to turn it into a huge hall of mirrors, which was *de rigueur* at the time. After this encounter with optical illusion, the visitor experienced the delights of acoustics on entering a deep grotto, where he heard sounds and harmonies but could not tell where they came from. Outside, beside a minaret, was a Tartar tent and a camel being led around by a servant dressed as a Turk. There was a white marble temple, a naumachia inspired by the one at the Villa of Hadrian, and a pyramid, all leading the visitor to profound nostalgia—though this was quickly forgotten, for it was all mere amusement.

When Carmontelle published a series of engravings of his extraordinary creation in 1779, the year after its completion, he provided the best justification for building the gardens: "If someone wishes to turn a picturesque garden into a land of illusion, why object to it? Illusion is the only way we can amuse ourselves; if Freedom and Art are the guide of this illusion, we will never be too far away from Nature."[13]

The receptions held at the Folie Monceau and the Folie d'Artois attracted the whole of the aristocracy, but they also attracted a certain amount of envy. Claude Baudard de Saint-James was particularly guilty of this sin. He was the treasurer of the French navy and had added the name of his village, Saint-Gemmes-Sur-Loire, to his surname, spelling it Saint James to make him sound more English.

In 1772 he had bought a tract of land near what was to be the comte d'Artois's home at Neuilly. Once d'Artois had built his folly, Claude de Saint-James decided he wanted one for himself. It touched his vanity to live so close to a princely residence and to outdo it in splendor. He asked François Bélanger to carry out his desires, saying that he could build whatever he wanted as long as it was expensive.[14] Bélanger spared no expense. After building a beautiful Italianate residence on two levels, opening onto the gardens via a graceful loggia, he designed gardens containing a great variety of buildings, with novelty and, more important, expenditure being the two main criteria.

The greatest of these follies, and the one the owner took most pride in, was a huge rock hiding a porch with six Doric columns and a huge bathroom, magnificently decorated with a ceiling of caissons and stucco rosettes. The nymphaeum, with a cascade flowing from it, was reflected in a basin to add to its classical grandeur. To create this particular folly Bélanger had huge blocks of sandstone transported from the forests of Fontainebleau by teams of forty horses. This alone cost Saint-James 1,600,000 *livres*.

When the work was complete, some marveled at the great number of outbuildings, but many thought the gardens were in poor taste. The Prince de Ligne, whom Bélanger had worked for on modifications to his residence at Beloeil, wrote in 1781: "Near Neuilly, there is a garden that would be extremely fine if there were not too much of it. Had he spent less money, Monsieur de Saint-James would have had more success. There are too many buildings too close together, but he can be excused in view of the good taste to be found among them."[15]

Claude de Saint-James had little time to enjoy the pleasures of his Anglo-Chinese gardens, for in 1787 he was imprisoned for debt. When he left prison, his residence had been sold cheaply to the duc de Choiseul-Praslin, a friend of his rival, the comte d'Artois.

Between 1775 and 1785, other wealthy landowners, such as Nicolas Beaujon, most of whom had acquired their colossal wealth from sea trading, transformed the gardens surrounding their homes into *parcs de curiosité*, rivaling the great princely follies. "But are gardens made to have tours conducted around them? Should we expect a spectacle when we visit a garden? It is only when those tiresome people return to their towns that one can enjoy a walk in these gardens."[16]

At the time the Prince de Ligne was reflecting on these lines, the extravagances of the likes of the duc de Chartres or the comte d'Artois, as well as the financiers who tried to outdo them, were not unanimously appreciated. The fashion of creating so many diversions and amusements to the total exclusion of any form

ABOVE: The Temple d'Amour at Trianon
OPPOSITE: View of the Cascade at Méréville
Jean-Joseph de Laborde, *Description des nouveaux Jardins de France*, 1808–16

of proper landscape gardening was often criticized. But most of the large houses of the time still had traditional gardens, though they were increasingly falling into disrepair.

> Everything in them is beautiful, and the eye is delighted, but this delight soon passes. . . . The trees look tired, the hedgerows droop, the paths are too churned up to walk on, the grass is unhealthy, not neat lawns but straggling hay. . . . I forgot the ridiculous plants, the designs, the festoons, the sad decorative hedges with no common theme, all enclosed by a wall that hides the surrounding countryside.[17]

From 1774 to 1781 painters, writers, and even the owners themselves, all under the banner of Thomas Whately's famous treatise, finally taught people how to take their inspiration from the gardens of England, but without resorting to the excesses of Anglo-Chinese follies.[18] They had a single principle in common: They took nature as their model, with all its changes from one season to another and the infinite variety to be obtained from properly designing the site.

The theorist Jean-Marie Morel, a specialist in this era of change in the art of the garden, wrote: "This art is not intended to produce an artificial design, but to order its gardens to conform with the rules set down by nature herself."[19] For the painter Claude-Henri Watelet, imitating nature involved subjugating it to art. In his *Essai sur les jardins,* published in 1774, the artist gave three essential characteristics on which every design should be based: the picturesque, the poetic, and the romantic. The gardener creates the picturesque by making every view in a garden pleasant:

> He will use all the resources of his art to lay out paths in an intelligent, attractive way. He will use meanderings in these paths to create distance between the garden and the spectator or to bring them closer together, depending on the purpose of the design, and by taking care to offer the spectator rest and repose, thereby drawing to his attention those features that are most important in his work.[20]

The scenes offered to the visitor naturally created varied emotions, for they offer in turn scenes that are noble, rustic, pleasant, cheerful, sad, or serious, like the scenes of a pastoral landscape.

The careful use of temples, rotundas, and inscriptions gave these gardens their poetic character, for by alluding to other gardens and other periods in history they could lead to renewed reflection and the most profound emotions. But Watelet was skeptical about these "poetic accessories": "They may add to the pleasures experienced by those with a flexible imagination or who are men of the world, but it must be agreed that to the greater number of people they are no more than curiosities."[21]

If the art of painting governs the composition of the garden, and if poetry calls to mind scenes through the use of architectural references, the romantic more particularly appeals to the world of the emotions: "Romantic ideas are more vague, more personal; they belong, as it were, to the individual more than to the crowd."[22] To create this romantic character, Watelet suggested that the artifices used by William Chambers to create scenes full of dread still be used, but he warned "the decorators of gardens" not to use these features to excess, for they "tend more directly to unsettle the imagination and create aberrations of taste."[23]

This picturesque, poetic view of the garden allowed it to be laid out along the lines of the English garden, but it introduced an additional benefit. Because illusion was created to evoke sensitivity and emotion, the garden could exercise its charms on the spectator without the designer using excessive artifice. The garden was still a piece of theater, but as Watelet wrote, "The new ways of decorating the garden are more reminiscent of a scene from the living theater than a motionless tableau."[24]

A CHANGE IN TASTES

Artists and designers were again beginning to turn for inspiration to Italy, the land where the finest landscapes were to be found. But they no longer sought ideal beauty, which the English sought so avidly. French artists recalled with a certain nostalgia the sites in Italy, which were both tangible and yet unreal, for they were all that remained of a greatness that had disappeared forever.

The drawings of Fragonard and Hubert Robert—in which time seems to stand still in a landscape of ruins overrun with vegetation and the only evidence of human life is a few shepherds—made during their stays at the Villa d'Este in the summer of 1761 were much in demand among collectors. Fragonard's drawings were published as a collection of engravings by the Abbé de Saint-Non in 1765, and they fascinated lovers of the picturesque. In the drawings, they found "among the images of thatched cottages and ruins a delightful repose that freed them from the search for that which was useful and from a preoccupation with social rank; this was a world where nothing happens, where things were simply a subject for contemplation."[25]

Princes and princesses began to order their painters or architects—the function of the master gardener was simply to work to their design—to turn part of an estate that was *à la française* into one that was *à l'anglaise*. The English garden was becoming more ethereal, like the landscapes of Italy. Gardens began to assume an insubstantial, inconsequential appearance, reflecting the semirealization that they were only there for games and festivities, where there was no thought for the morrow.

THE NATURAL ILLUSION

At Chantilly, from 1772 to 1773, the prince de Condé had his architect, Julien-David Leroy, redesign in the English style the woodland to the right of his château along the Grand Canal. The following year Marie-Antoinette, who had just moved into the Petit Trianon, ordered her master gardener, Claude Richard, to produce plans for a park in the style of the day, to replace Louis XV's former botanical gardens. But when the young gardener proposed a garden she found excessively Anglo-Chinese, she went to the comte de Caraman for advice, for he had managed to give his gardens in Roissy "an English note created with infinite skill and good taste."[26]

With the aid of the queen's chief architect, Richard Mique, the count designed a garden of broad, harmonious lines, which the queen accepted in 1777. The whole design is based around two adjoining landscapes along a meandering stream, which appears to be flowing from a picturesque rock. The queen asked for fourteen different designs for this artificial grotto but finally chose the design produced by Hubert Robert, the only one she liked. This was built in 1781. Two years before, Robert had produced the interior for the magnificent Basin of Apollo for the gardens at Versailles, a new Palace of Thetis, where a splendid grotto shelters the sun god and his nymphs and chariot.

At the Trianon, the grotto was much smaller. A stone bridge led to a small belvedere, an octagonal music pavilion built by Richard Mique. Just after this, the visitor finds the second sight created for him by the architect: the Temple de l'Amour, a small rotunda with a portico of twenty-two white marble pillars, its melancholy reflection seen in the waters of the surrounding stream. Work on the gardens at the Trianon was not completed until 1782, and the queen and her court loved to hold open-air festivals there, ending with magnificent illuminations.

In 1778, Marie-Antoinette inaugurated the Temple de l'Amour with a magnificent buffet held under the trellised bowers specially built for the occasion. In the afternoon, Italian plays were presented in an open-air theater, and in the evening the gardens were lit by 1,800 lanterns. Every visit by a foreign sovereign—Grand Duke Paul of Russia, Gustave III of Sweden, and Archduke Ferdinand, Governor of Lombardy, to name but three—was an excuse for another reception at the Trianon. The queen's favorite painter, Claude-Louis Châtelet, produced many canvases depicting the festivities, and when these reached the courts of Austria and Germany, they, too, developed a taste for the new "picturesque" gardens.

Even before the Petit Trianon was finished, members of the French royal family were following Marie-Antoinette's example. The duc de Penthièvre ordered his architect, Paindebled, to turn part of his estate at Rambouillet into gardens with a grotto, cascade, and a stream beside which weeping willows trailed their branches. To enhance the visual attraction of the gardens, a thatched cottage was built between two arms of the stream. Although the exterior of the cottage looked simple, the interior was ornately decorated with shells in a way similar to the nymphaea of the previous century.

Near Versailles, at Montreuil, the comtesse de Provence, sister-in-law to the king, invited her architect, Jean-François Chalgrin, to extend the indoor *trompe l'oeil* garden of her music pavilion, again in the style of the day. In the same year, 1780, she was followed by Madame de Balbi, the comte de Provence's "favorite," and Mesdames de France, the king's aunts, who asked Charles Lesage to design new gardens for them at the Château de Bellevue.

A lake, a pond, or a slow, meandering stream always served as a guide through these gardens of illusion. Their banks were a place for the *promenade,* a pastime that was rapidly gaining in popularity.

Rousseau, who had just published *Les Rêveries d'un Promeneur,* was being rediscovered, and people began reading *La Nouvelle Héloïse* again. Now the supreme

C'EST UN FILS MONSIEUR!

artifice for a woman was to appear natural, not only by taking pleasure in the rediscovery of nature but in the new way of life she espoused, where the joys of motherhood were once again being affirmed. Restif de la Bretonne wrote *Vrais plaisirs ou des délices de la maternité*,[27] and many pictures were produced depicting the "good husband" handing his child over to his young wife to be suckled.[28]

The countryside was no longer viewed purely as landscape. Country activities were also worthy of imitation—the very model of an ideal society—though people were also aware of the realities of country life, not least the poverty that still ruled there.

Hamlets and sheepfolds began to appear in the gardens of princes. Watelet's book had begun with a section on useful accoutrements for a garden and emphasized the importance of the arrangement of various farm buildings within the design: stables, granaries, dairies, and beehives, all designed to use nature's benefits for profit, "for the pleasures of the countryside should be a fabric of desires aroused without affectation and satisfactions provided without effort."[29]

The idea of the ornamental farm also originated in England. Between 1732 and 1745 the poet William Shenstone created a model farm garden at the Leasowes, his estate in Shropshire. He himself played a major part in its layout, attempting to reproduce the rural ideal in concrete form, as the ancients themselves conceived of it.

Between Colombes and Argenteuil, near Paris, Watelet had already added farm buildings to the estate he bought in 1754: a dairy and a little windmill, which was the origin of the name of the estate, "Moulin-Joli." His friends François Boucher and Hubert Robert would go there to draw, attracted by the idyllic charm of the painter's design.

Moulin-Joli is very much the vision of a painter, and it is the techniques of the painter that create emotion in the visitor. The prince de Ligne himself was very taken with the illusion produced by the aesthetic pleasures of the garden: "If your hearts are not hardened, sit down between the arms of a willow at Moulin-Joli, on the edge of the stream. Read, watch, and weep, but with delight, not sadness. You will see the image of your soul."[30]

The prince de Condé was the first to follow in Watelet's footsteps by building a Norman-style hamlet at Chantilly in 1775. The hamlet consists of seven small buildings, including a mill, barn, and farmhouse surrounding a small area of lawn. And in 1780 Mesdames de France at Bellevue, Madame de Provence at Montreuil, and the comte d'Artois at Raincy all succumbed to the idea of the rustic garden.

In 1782 Marie-Antoinette ordered her own rustic garden from Richard Mique and Hubert Robert, where a mill, dairy, aviary, barn, and farmhouse were built around the queen's house and were reflected in a small lake. A belvedere, known as Marlborough's Tower (after the song repopularized by Beaumarchais, *"Marlborough s'en va-t-en guerre"*), gave a bird's-eye view of a garden where all was artifice, even the cracks in the walls of the houses, and which was not finished until 1789, when "the wolves were walking into the sheepfold."[31]

After buying Monsieur de Penthièvre's estates at Rambouillet, Louis XVI also began to take an interest in rural life, but in less idyllic fashion than the queen. Many landowners had heard about the new intensive agriculture being practiced in England and took a great interest in it themselves. On his new estate, the king created an experimental farm for breeding merino sheep, and as an encouragement to the queen to come and visit it, he also ordered Thévenin to build him a dairy, whose surroundings were to be landscaped by Hubert Robert. Through its porch with two pillars resembling a temple, the dairy opens onto a cool room made of marble, and a second offers the sight of the nymph Amalthea, sculpted by Pierre Julien, in a great grotto.

The *laiterie,* or queen's dairy, encouraged the queen and her entourage to eat "a pastoral repast, composed principally of milk and a few fruits" on the great marble table in the first hall.[32] But Marie-Antoinette preferred to play the role of farmer's wife at the Trianon, where the bowls in the dairy were specially made by Sèvres, and none of the smells of the farmyard troubled her nostrils.

The attraction of pleasures that neither the town nor society could provide led more than one person to carry out "particularly in spring, the project of creating a pastoral retreat. This was a romantic ideal, like that of love, of success and fortune, which everyone had at the back of his mind."[33] The aristocrat or rich landowner could withdraw from the world so as to show his soul in a better light: "It will be a public act of confidence, a statement that everyone will be able to read."[34] Every guest and visitor could see the sentiments of the owner being expressed in a garden of visible illusion, his thoughts revealed by the careful use of particular features in the garden, always arranged along a stream or around a

LES VRAIS PLAISIRS

OPPOSITE: It's a Boy, Monsieur!
ABOVE: The True Pleasures or Delights of
Maternity
Nicolas Restif de la Bretonne, *Tableaux de la Vie ou Moeurs du XVIIIᵉ siècle*, 1791

pond or small lake. The visitor would find inscriptions that would cause him to ponder on past civilizations, or he might suddenly discover a tomb. "It is not enough to delight the eye, one must speak to the heart,"[35] stated the Abbé Delille, the new guide to these gardens of sensitivity.

The same thought was shared by René Louis de Girardin, a captain in the king of Poland's guard. He had been exiled to Lunéville, where in 1770 he began rebuilding the family home at Ermenonville. He made several visits to England, and the great sweeping lines of his gardens were modeled on Stourhead.

The gardens in front of the château were remodeled to emphasize the lake they surrounded. A small stream known as "La Launette" crossed the whole estate and led the walker along its banks. An island planted with poplar trees surrounding a tomb was the next thing to catch the eye. This captured the essence of the gardens, for it was the tomb of Jean-Jacques Rousseau. The philosopher had returned to Paris in 1767 and was living there under a false name. In 1778 he was invited by the marquis de Girardin to spend the summer at Ermenonville. But barely two months after he arrived, on July 2, he died while returning home from a walk in the country. The marquis was shattered. He asked Hubert Robert to redesign the area and make it the eternal resting place of his famous guest. The job of building a tomb was given to the sculptor Le Sueur. René de Girardin had found the perfect communion between nature and the human mind by burying Rousseau here, even though in 1794 his ashes were moved to the Panthéon.

Even in the first designs for the gardens, Girardin had wanted the water, the meadows, and the woods to serve the sole purpose of further refining the noble thoughts aroused by the ornamental buildings, columns, and inscriptions. The unfinished Temple de la Philosophie, dedicated to Montaigne, is an injunction to accept "the imperfections of human knowledge," which existed even among history's greatest thinkers—Newton, Descartes, Voltaire, and Rousseau—to whom the broken columns around the little temple are dedicated. Other less formal but more sentimental buildings were scattered around the garden: the *banc des mères de famille*, the *banc de la reine*, and the tomb of the painter Johann Prokop Mayer.

To the north of the house, the estate was extended by a large lake and an area of stony wasteland where all that grew was some heather and where "the hand of man had taken care not to profane nature."[36] Further on, the Monument des Anciennes Amours recalls the impossible love of Julie and Saint-Preux.

Between 1770 and 1780, at the same time as Girardin was redesigning Ermenonville, not far away Le Pelletier de Mortefontaine, the administrator of Soissons, was also redesigning his estates to turn them into an image of a distant Arcadia. Here also the visitor was led along a river toward a huge rock, on which were inscribed the verses of the Abbé Delille: "Its indestructible mass has tired time itself."

This deliberate air of melancholy was quite the opposite of what François-Nicolas Racine de Monville, the "Grand Master of the Water and Forests of Rouen," intended when he moved into his new home at Retz, near the village of Chambourcy, in 1774. Monsieur de Monville typified the age in which he lived, for he had been left a huge fortune by his grandfather and was an expert botanist, a talented musician, an accomplished sportsman, and a respected socialite. He did not want his estates to create romantic reveries or to amuse or enchant like the Anglo-Chinese follies of the duc de Chartres and the comte d'Artois. His sole desire was to refine his own and his guests' sensibilities by means of the great proving ground that is nature, expressed in the sophisticated use of the various features of the design and by placing them carefully so as to form a kind of "personal autobiography."[37]

A dark grotto, lit by two giant torch-bearing satyrs, heralds the Désert de Retz, as many places for retirement or country leisure belonging to the wealthy were then known. As the visitor wanders through the gardens, he discovers apparently by chance a Chinese house, based on designs by William Chambers, an open-air theater, a pyramidal icehouse, the Temple of Pan, and the ruins of a thirteenth-century Gothic church purchased from the nearby village. But the gardens are dominated by a huge and extraordinary broken column, the Column House, in which Monsieur de Monville set up his apartments in 1780, its interior laid out in exceptionally good taste.

By the time this unusual country retreat was finished, de Monville was spending months at a time at Retz, where he loved to receive painters and men of letters and to oversee his gardens, which he had had planted with many exotic and domestic plants. His greenhouses were so famous that when the assets of the estate were sold off during the Revolution, all the rare plants they contained were taken to the Jardin des Plantes.

In Retz, too, the spirit of Italy was ever present. The power of the deliberately ruined column, bathed in the light of the Ile de France, which gave the whole scene an air of unreality, and the presence of the Temple of Pan and the pyramid, recalling the tombs of the Via Appia, inevitably called to mind the views Hubert Robert brought back from Rome, and more especially those of Piranesi, which the architect Pierre-Adrien Pâris had played a large part in introducing to France.

Painters who could re-create the idyllic vision reminiscent of Italy were in increasing demand, in particular Hubert Robert, who was able to attain this subtle harmony between sky, water, the foliage of the countryside, and ancient ruins. In 1780 the princesse de Monaco asked Robert to redesign her gardens at Betz. On the banks of "La Grivette" the painter planned an abandoned feudal castle and a Vallée des Tombeaux. Before the visitor's sadness became too overwhelming, he was led to the Pavillon du Repos. At the Temple de l'Amitié, a sense of peace gradually returned to the spectator as he realized the futility of amorous passion— the princesse de Monaco had been infatuated with the prince de Condé—for only the deepest emotions will last, and nature provides the clearest evidence of this fact. The deaths of Julie, of Werther and Virginie, all victims of impossible love, haunt these gardens.

Memory, nostalgia, and the worship of a loved one were the favorite subjects for the last of the gardens of illusion. When Jean-Joseph de Laborde, at the age of sixty, bought the Château de Méréville in the valley of the Juine, he declared that it was to be a place for him to live out the last years of his life in peace and tranquillity, seeking to preserve forever the illusion of a lost world. The architect to whom he gave this task, François-Joseph Bélanger, was more used to working on the comte D'Artois's follies. Bélanger initially planned to make the gardens a pastoral retreat in the tradition of Watelet, with windmills, little bridges, and fishermen's cottages. But this was not what Laborde had in mind, so he went instead to Hubert Robert.

At Méréville the painter created a landscape whose harmony nothing could disturb: Buildings like the Temple of Filial Piety and the dairy transported the visitor to a different world. But the monument to English navigator Captain James Cook, sculpted by Augustin Pajou, and the column by Martin Leprince, built in memory of the owner's two sons who had died in a shipwreck, cast a dark cloud over this excessively Arcadian vision. As work on the château drew to a close, its owner was already worrying about the Revolution, and during the Terror, in 1794, Laborde went to the scaffold. In 1819 the estate was sold and Méréville was lost, but at the end of the century it was re-created on a neighboring estate, the Parc de Jeurre. Its owner, the comte de Saint-Léon, built his own home in 1891 in the image of Laborde's.

At the end of the eighteenth century, one last person tried to re-create the beauty of Italy on his own land in France. This was the baron de Castille, who returned to his estate at Uzès after many trips to Florence, Rome, and Campania, where he had spent considerable time at the ruins of Paestum. Shortly afterward, he wrote to the comtesse d'Albany: "I have acquired such a taste for the columns of Italy that I have just created four monopteral temples to lighten the solitude of my gardens. I have created here that which I saw and liked so much elsewhere; every scene in my gardens now includes something man-made . . . a water basin surrounded by columns, a well shaped like a temple; all that I have created is in miniature."[38] All over the surrounding countryside, in the fields and woods, he built columns, often in memory of people he had known; as well as peristyles for his wife's mausoleum, grouped in threes and topped with a crescent for his son, who was killed at the Battle of Essing.

Soon, all these illusions would fade into the distance and nostalgia would give way to reason. The garden, as it brought people closer to nature, would

Pierre-Louis de la Rive
Tomb of Suzanne de la Rive
Oil, 1787

teach us that we are ephemeral, that we will pass on as generations before us have passed on, that wisdom lies in the acceptance of the passing seasons and the vicissitudes of life. We must make way for others to become spectators of the wonders of creation. . . . Nature, the source of human genius . . . leads us in ecstasy to the idea of ruin and the decay of matter. Our final delight is in abandoning ourselves to death, an exaltation that anticipates the darkness into which we will vanish.[39]

The folly of "folies,"

Bagatelle, Paris
The comte d'Artois's "Folie," 1777
François-Joseph Bélanger, architect
RIGHT: Sphinx on the steps leading to the gardens
BELOW: The side of the building facing onto the
ceremonial courtyard
OPPOSITE, ABOVE: The garden side of the building

OPPOSITE, BELOW: Elevation of Bagatelle from the
side of the building by the ceremonial courtyard
François-Joseph Bélanger, *Les Plans du château,
cours et jardins de Bagatelle*, 1777

1

2

3

A wager by the comte d'Artois

4

The gold of Bagatelle

*Is the Bois de Boulogne not enhanced by the presence of a
great prince? Bagatelle is the prettiest bauble in the world.
The drawing rooms, the mahogany staircase, the fine
environs; everything there is pleasing, everything delightful.*

Charles-Joseph, Prince de Ligne,
Coup d'oeil sur Beloeil, 1781

Bagatelle, Paris
The comte d'Artois's "Folie," 1777
Decorations in the Salon Rond, 1777–79
Stucco by Nicolas-François Lhullier
Painting and gilding by Daniel Aubert
Arabesque designs by Jean-Marie Dussaux
Trompe-l'oeil cameo by Jean Démosthène Dugourc

A passing fancy:

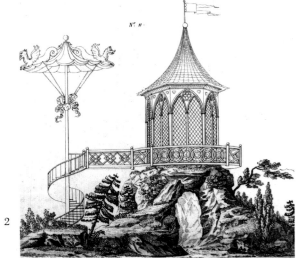

Bagatelle gardens, Paris, 1777–86
Thomas Blaikie
ABOVE: Trellised summerhouse

RIGHT: Bagatelle gardens (detail)
J. C. Kraft, *Receuil d'Architecture civile*, 1804

4

Antoine-Patrice Guillot
View of the Mill at the Folie Beaujon
Oil, 1827

Anglo-Chinese gardens;

5

Jean-Honoré Fragonard
Festivities at Rambouillet or the Ile d'Amour
Oil, c. 1780

1

$\mathcal{A}$ *new*

fashion:

2

3

The illusion of

the picturesque . . .

4

The gardens of Versailles, 1662–87
OPPOSITE, BELOW: Basin of Apollo, 1774–79
Designed by Hubert Robert, built by Thévenin

Petit Trianon Gardens, Versailles, 1777–81
Comte de Caraman and Richard Mique
ABOVE: Rock, 1781

Bagatelle gardens, Paris, 1777–86
LEFT: Chinese rock

Idyllic gardens,

Petit Trianon Gardens, Versailles, 1777–81
OPPOSITE: Temple de l'Amour, 1778
Richard Mique
BELOW: Belvedere Pavilion, 1781
Richard Mique

Claude-Louis Châtelet
Illumination of the Belvedere Pavilion for Emperor Joseph II
Oil, 1781

2

3

Nicolas Lavrience
Festivities at Trianon for Gustave III of Sweden
Gouache, 1784

4

Where there is no tomorrow . . .

To create the illusion of a return to nature,

4

5

Ermenonville, Oise
Gardens of Marquis René-Louis de Girardin, 1766–80
OPPOSITE, ABOVE, LEFT: Memorial column
OPPOSITE, BELOW: Temple of Philosophy
ABOVE: Island of Poplars with the tomb of
Jean-Jacques Rousseau
Hubert Robert and Jacques Lesueur, 1779
LEFT: Pont de la Brasserie

OPPOSITE, ABOVE, RIGHT: The Philosopher's Pyramid
at Ermenonville
Jean-Joseph de Laborde, *Description des nouveaux
Jardins de France*, 1808–16

And to live the illusion of pastoral life.

2

Petit Trianon Gardens, Versailles, 1777–81
The Hamlet, 1782–89
Designed by Hubert Robert, built by Richard Mique
OPPOSITE: Marlborough's Tower
ABOVE: The Queen's House

BELOW: The Cow Farm at Raincy
Jean-Joseph de Laborde, *Description des nouveaux Jardins de France*, 1808–16

3

Rambouillet, Yvelines
English gardens of the château and seashell cottage
Designed for the duc de Penthièvre by Paindebled,
1779–80
BELOW: Exterior view
ABOVE AND OPPOSITE: Details of the interior

A thatched cottage for a princess . . .

A dairy for a queen . . .

1

Rambouillet, Yvelines
The Queen's Dairy, 1785–88
Designed by Thévenin
Interior decoration by Pierre Julien
RIGHT: Facade
ABOVE AND OPPOSITE, BELOW: The nymph Amalthaea in
the salle de fraîcheur

OPPOSITE, ABOVE: Charles Percier
Section through the Dairy at Rambouillet
Pen, wash, and gouache, c. 1790

2

3

4

1

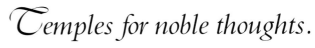
Temples for noble thoughts.

2

3

4

Parc de Jeurre, Essone
Ornamental buildings in the Méréville Gardens,
1785–93
Designed for Jean-Joseph de Laborde by
François-Joseph Bélanger and Hubert Robert
OPPOSITE, ABOVE: Monument to James Cook,
1786–90
OPPOSITE, BELOW: Dairy, 1790–93
ABOVE: Temple of Filial Piety, 1786–89

LEFT: Temple at Méréville
Jean-Joseph de Laborde, *Description des nouveaux
Jardins de France*, 1808–16

Temple au Dieu Pan.

1

The final illusions:

3

2

Désert de Retz, Chambourcy
Estate of Monsieur de Monville, 1774–89
LEFT: Temple of Pan
ABOVE AND OPPOSITE, ABOVE: Broken column

TOP: Temple of Pan at Retz
OPPOSITE, BELOW: Perspective view of the column
at Retz
Le Rouge, *Les Jardins Anglo-Chinois
à la Mode*, 1776–89

4

Forcing nature into submission . . .

5

1

Domaine de Castille, Uzès, Gard
Gardens laid out by G. Joseph de Froment,
baron of Castille, 1794–1823
ABOVE: Outbuildings designed to resemble a
porticoed temple
OPPOSITE: Semicircular ruins marking the entrance
to the château

RIGHT: Giovanni Paolo Pannini
Ruins of an Ancient Roman Temple
Etching by François-Philippe Charpentier, 1761

2

And fixing eternity in stone . . .

Dispersed through all the thinning dust there loom
The baths, the palaces, the Caesar's tombs,
While Virgil's, Ovid's, Horace's footprints now
Imagination only can with life endow.
Happy one hundred times, who builds a park
And imitates these relics through his art.
For now time's silent hand comes to his aid
Already Mother Nature's mark is made
On these memorials of another age.

Abbé Delille, *Les Jardins*, 1786

NOTES

CHAPTER 1
THE PATH TO INITIATION *(pages 1–31)*

1. André Chastel, *Le mythe de la Renaissance, 1420–1520* (Geneva, 1969).
2. Leon Battista Alberti, *De re aedificatoria* (written between 1447 and 1455) (Florence, 1485). Reprinted in Manfredo Tafuri, *Architecture et Humanisme de la Renaissance aux réformes* (Paris, 1981).
3. Ibid.
4. Emanuela Kretzulesco-Quaranta, *Les jardins du Songe: Poliphile et la mystique de la Renaissance*, French edition (Paris, 1976).
5. Michel Melot, *L'Illustration* (Geneva, 1984).
6. André Chastel, *La crise de la Renaissance, 1520–1600* (Geneva, 1968).
7. Michel de Montaigne, *Journal de voyage en Italie par la Suisse et l'Allemagne, 1580–1581* (Complete works, Paris, 1962).
8. Francesco Colonna, *Hypnérotomachie ou Discours du Songe de Poliphile* (Paris, 1546).
9. Ibid.
10. Ibid.
11. Jacqueline Theurillat, *Les mystères de Bomarzo et les jardins symboliques de la Renaissance* (Geneva, 1973).
12. Christiane Gil, *Bianca Capello* (Paris, 1983).
13. Vicino Orsini, *Lettre de Vicino Orsini au cardinal Alessandro Farnese* (Bomarzo, 1563). Reprinted in Theurillat, *Les mystères de Bomarzo.*
14. Chastel, *La crise de la Renaissance.*
15. Kretzulesco-Quaranta, *Les jardins du Songe.*
16. Ibid.
17. Charles De Brosses, *Lettres historiques et critiques sur l'Italie* (Paris, 1799).
18. Colonna, *Hypnérotomachie.*
19. Ibid.

CHAPTER 2
THE PATH TO KNOWLEDGE *(pages 32–61)*

1. Francesco Colonna, *Hypnérotomachie ou Discours du Songe de Poliphile* (Paris, 1546).
2. Ibid.
3. Marguerite Charageat, *L'art des jardins* (Paris, 1962).
4. Pietro de' Crescenzi, chapter 8 in *Le livre des prouffits champestres et ruraux*, 2 vols. (Lyons, 1530).
5. *Le Roman de la Rose*, an allegorical romance in two parts. Guillaume de Lorris is the author of the first part, written around 1236; Jean de Meun wrote the second between 1275 and 1280.
6. Jacques Dupont and Cesare Gnudi, *La peinture gothique* (Geneva, 1954).
7. "A garden inclosed is my sister, my spouse; a spring shut up, a fountain sealed. . . . A fountain of gardens, a well of living waters, and streams from Lebanon." Song of Solomon 14:12–15.
8. André Chastel, *Le mythe de la Renaissance, 1420–1520* (Geneva, 1969).
9. Jean Orieux, *Catherine de Médicis* (Paris, 1986).
10. Etienne Barilier, *Le dixième Ciel* (Paris, 1986).
11. Charageat, *L'art des jardins.*
12. Michel Brunet, "Le parc d'attractions des Ducs de Bourgogne à Hesdin," in *Gazette des Beaux-Arts* (Paris, 1971).
13. André Félibien, *Mémoires pour servir à l'histoire des maisons royalles et bastiments de France, 1681 . . .* (Paris, 1874).
14. Robert Carvallo, *Villandry et ses jardins* (Colmar-Ingersheim, 1978).
15. Orieux, *Catherine de Médicis.*
16. Jacques Androuet Du Cerceau, *Les Plus Excellents Bastiments de France*, 2 vols. (Paris, 1576–79).
17. Orieux, *Catherine de Médicis.*
18. William Howard Adams, *The French Garden, 1500–1800* (New York, 1979).
19. Ibid. See Ronsard, *Eglogue III, Chant pastoral sur les Noces de Monseigneur Charles, duc de Lorraine, et Madame Claude, fille deuxième du roi Henri II* (1559).
20. Ernest de Ganay, *Les jardins de France et leur décor* (Paris, 1949).
21. André Du Chesne, *Antiquités et recherches des villes, chasteaux . . .* (1602). Reprinted in Ganay, *Les jardins de France.*
22. Axelle de Gaigneron, "Les eaux vives qui entretiennent—côté jardin—la renommée fastueuse de Vaux-le-Vicomte," in *Connaissance des Arts* (Paris, 1976).

23. Thetis was a goddess of the sea, daughter of Nereus, and mother of Achilles. Tethys was a Titan, daughter of Uranus and wife of the sea god Oceanus. According to the *Encyclopédie Larousse*, 'Thetis' is a corrupted spelling, adopted by artists to refer to Tethys in depicting the sun visiting the empire of the sea, as in the group sculpted by Girardon, Regnaudin, Marsy, and Guérin for the *Grotte de Thétis* at Versailles.

CHAPTER 3
GARDENS TO DAZZLE THE EYE *(pages 62–95)*

1. Translations of treatises on architecture by Jean Martin: L.B. Alberti, *De l'Architecture* (Paris, 1553); S. Serlio, *Le Premier Livre d'architecture (Le Second Livre de perspective)* . . . (Paris, 1545); Vitruvius, *L'Architecture ou art de bien bâtir* . . . (Paris, 1547).
2. Treatises by Jacques Androuet Du Cerceau: *Les Grotesques* . . . (1566); *Le Premier, le Second et le Troisième Livre d'architecture* (Paris, 1559–61 and 1572); *Les Plus Excellents Bastiments de France* (Paris, 1576–79).
3. William Howard Adams, *The French Garden, 1500–1800* (New York, 1979).
4. Jean Orieux, *Catherine de Médicis* (Paris, 1986).
5. Ibid.
6. Ibid.
7. Ernest de Ganay, *Les jardins de France et leur décor* (Paris, 1949).
8. Jacques Boyceau de la Baraudière, *Traité du Jardinage selon les raisons de la nature et de l'art* (Paris, 1638).
9. Ibid.
10. Ibid.
11. Marguerite Charageat, *L'art des jardins* (Paris, 1962).
12. Bernard Jeannel, *Le Nôtre* (Paris, 1985).
13. François Crouzet, "Versailles," in *Spectacles du Monde* (1986).
14. Saint-Simon, "Mémoires," in Jeannel, *Le Nôtre*.
15. Jeannel, *Le Nôtre*.
16. Jean Starobinski, *L'invention de la liberté* (Geneva, 1964).
17. Mademoiselle de Scudéry, *La promenade de Versailles* (Paris, 1669).
18. Pierre Gaxotte, *La France de Louis XIV* (Paris, 1946).
19. Benoist-Méchin, *L'homme et ses jardins ou les métamorphoses du Paradis terrestre* (Paris, 1975).
20. André Félibien, *Les divertissements de Versailles* . . . (Paris, 1674).
21. Benoist-Méchin, *L'homme et ses jardins*.
22. Saint-Simon, *Mémoires* (Paris, 1959–61).
23. Ibid.
24. Ibid.
25. Carlo Vanvitelli, Luigi's son, finished the cascade at Caserta for Ferdinand IV in 1759, when he succeeded Charles VII, who became king of Spain under the title Charles III.

CHAPTER 4
THE LIBERTARIAN ITINERARY *(pages 96–127)*

1. Jean Starobinski, *L'invention de la liberté* (Geneva, 1964).
2. Ibid.
3. Ibid.
4. William Howard Adams, *The French Garden, 1500–1800* (New York, 1979).
5. Starobinski, *L'invention de la liberté*.
6. Benoist-Méchin, *L'homme et ses jardins ou les métamorphoses du Paradis terrestre* (Paris, 1975).
7. John Locke, *An Essay Concerning Human Understanding* (1690).
8. Antoine-Joseph Dezallier D'Argenville, *La Théorie et la Pratique du Jardinage* (The Hague, 1715).
9. Marguerite Charageat, *L'art des jardins* (Paris, 1962).
10. André Mollet, *Le jardin de plaisir* (Stockholm, 1651).
11. Jacques-François Blondel, *De la distribution des maisons de plaisance et de la décoration des édifices en général* (Paris, 1737).
12. Ibid.
13. Starobinski, *L'invention de la liberté*.
14. Blondel, *De la distribution des maisons*.
15. Starobinski, *L'invention de la liberté*.
16. Ibid.
17. Pierre Gaxotte, *Louis XV* (Paris, 1980).
18. Starobinski, *L'invention de la liberté*.
19. Blondel, *De la distribution des maisons*.
20. Antoine-Joseph Dezallier D'Argenville, *Voyage pittoresque des environs de Paris* (Paris, 1762).
21. Ibid.
22. Christopher Thacker, the Rococo garden in *The History of Gardens* (London, 1979).
23. Claude Arthaud, *Les palais du rêve* (Paris, 1970).
24. Thacker, *The History of Gardens*.

25. Starobinski, *L'invention de la liberté*.
26. Ibid.
27. Ibid.
28. Nicolas Le Camus de Mézières, *Le génie de l'architecture, ou l'analogie de cet art avec nos sensations* (Paris, 1780).
29. Jacques Wilhelm, "Les rapports artistiques avec l'Europe," in René Huyghe, *L'art et l'homme*, vol. 3 (Paris, 1961).
30. Starobinski, *L'invention de la liberté*.
31. Denis Diderot, *Les bijoux indiscrets* (Paris, 1747).
32. Starobinski, *L'invention de la liberté*.
33. Henry Soulange-Bodin, "La 'folie' du sieur Van Robais, Bagatelle," in *Le Figaro artistique* (November 1926).

CHAPTER 5
EXOTICISM *(pages 128–57)*

1. Voltaire, *Relation du bannissement dés Jesuites de la Chine* (Amsterdam, 1768).
2. M. de la Harpe, "Voyages, négociations et entreprises des Hollandais à la Chine," chapter 2 in *Abrégé de l'Histoire générale des voyages*, vol. 7 (Paris, 1780).
3. Ibid., chapter 1, "Précis des différents voyages à la Chine, depuis le XIIIe siècle jusqu'à nos jours."
4. Ibid.
5. Michel Beurdeley, "Un extravagant Versailles, version chinoise," in *Connaissance des Arts* (1957).
6. Jean-Denis Attiret, *Un récit particulier des jardins de l'Empereur de Chine* (1752); English translation by Sir H. Beaumont, *A Particular Account of the Emperor of China's Gardens Near Peking* (London, 1752). See also *Correspondance des missionaires portant sur les jardins de l'Empereur*: R. P. Louis le Comte, *Mémoires*, 9 vols. (1696); *Lettres édifiantes écrites des missions étrangères, 1717–1776*, 34 vols. (correspondence of Jesuit Fathers, including that of Father Attiret of 1743).
7. George Soulié de Morant, *L'épopée des Jésuites français en Chine, 1534–1928* (Paris, 1928).
8. Ibid.
9. Beurdeley, "Un extravagant Versailles."
10. Soulié de Morant, *L'épopée des Jésuits français*.
11. Ibid.
12. Jurgis Baltrusaitis, *Jardins, pays d'illusion*, preface to the catalogue of the exhibition *Jardins en France, 1760–1820*, organized by the Caisse nationale des Monuments historiques (Paris, 1977).
13. Dereck Clifford, *A History of Garden Design* (London, 1962).
14. William Chambers, *Designs of Chinese Buildings*, published in Georges-Louis Le Rouge, *Jardins Anglo-Chinois à la mode* (Paris, 1776–89).
15. Ibid.
16. Ibid.
17. Ibid.
18. Ibid.
19. Soulié de Morant, *L'épopée des Jésuits français*.
20. Henri-Paul Eydoux, *Monuments curieux et sites étranges* (Paris, 1974).
21. Nicolas Le Camus de Mézières, *Le génie de l'architecture, ou l'analogie de cet art avec nos sensations* (Paris, 1780).
22. Olivier Choppin de Janvry, "Le pavillon chinois de Cassan: Restauration et mise en valeur d'un témoin précieux de l'architecture des jardins du XVIIIe siècle," in *La Revue Française* (1975).

CHAPTER 6
THE ENCHANTING GARDEN *(pages 158–85)*

1. John Milton, *Paradise Lost*, Book IV (London, 1667).
2. Jean Starobinski, *L'invention de la liberté* (Geneva, 1964).
3. Sir William Temple, *Upon the Gardens of Epicurus, or of Gardening in the Year 1685*, Miscellanea, Part 2, in *Works*, vol. 2 (London, 1720).
4. Milton, *Paradise Lost*, Book IV.
5. Michel Le Bris, *Journal du Romanticisme* (Geneva, 1981).
6. Joseph Addison, in *The Spectator* (London), June–July 1712, no. 411–12
7. Ibid., no. 414.
8. Ibid., no. 416.
9. Anonymous, *Nouveau voyage d'Italie*, vol. 2, 5th ed. (The Hague, 1731).
10. First complete English edition of Andrea Palladio, *I Quattro Libri dell'Architettura* (1570): Giacomo Leoni, *I Quattro Libri* (London, 1715), followed by Colin Campbell, *Palladio's First Book of Architecture* (London, 1728), and Isaac Ware, *Palladio's Four Books of Architecture* (London, 1738).

11. Dereck Clifford, *A History of Garden Design* (London, 1962).
12. Christopher Hussey, *English Gardens and Landscapes, 1700–1750* (London, 1967).
13. Clifford, *L'Histoire et l'art des jardins*.
14. Horace Walpole, *Anecdotes of Painting in England . . . and Incidental Notes on Other Arts*, 4 vols. (London, 1762–80), vol. 4, *On Modern Gardening*. French translation by Louis-Jules-Barbon Mancini-Mazarini, duke of Nivernais, *Essai sur l'Art des jardins modernes* (Strawberry Hill, 1785).
15. Addison, in *The Spectator*.
16. William Gilpin, *A Dialogue upon the Gardens of the Right Honorable Lord Viscount Cobham at Stowe in Buckinghamshire* (London, 1749).
17. Ibid.
18. On the distribution of Lorrain drawings and Gaspar Dughet paintings in eighteenth-century English collections, see the introduction by Marie-Madeleine Martinet to *Art et Nature en Grande-Bretagne au XVIIIe siècle* (Paris, 1980).
19. Walpole, *Anecdotes of Painting in England*.
20. Alexander Pope, *Epistle IV to Lord Burlington* (1731).
21. Translation by Alexander Pope of a poem by Cardinal Bembo, given in his 1725 correspondence and adopted by Henry Flitcroft for the grotto at Stourhead.
22. William Mason, *The English Garden* (Dublin, 1782; book 1 published in 1772).
23. Clifford, *A History of Garden Design*.
24. Walpole, *Anecdotes of Painting in England*.
25. Thomas Whately, *Observations on Modern Gardening* (London, 1770). French translation by François-de-Paule Latapie, *L'art de former les jardins modernes, ou l'Art des jardins anglois* (Paris, 1771).
26. Ibid.
27. Le Bris, *Journal du Romanticisme*.

CHAPTER 7
THE GARDEN OF ILLUSION *(pages 186–221)*

1. Beatrice De Andia, "Folies, fêtes et favorites" in the catalogue of the exhibition *De Bagatelle à Monceau: Les Folies du XVIIIe siècle à Paris*, Domaine de Bagatelle and Musée Carnavalet (Paris 1978–79.)
2. René-Louis de Voyer de Paulmy, marquis d'Argenson, *Mémoires et Journal inédit du marquis d'Argenson*, annotated and published by his great-grandson, the marquis d'Argenson (Paris, 1857–58).
3. Jean Stern, *A l'ombre de Sophie Arnould, François-Joseph Bélanger* (Paris, 1930).
4. Marc-Antoine Laugier, *Essai sur l'architecture*, 2d ed. (Paris, 1755).
5. Jean-Jacques Rousseau, *Lettres de deux amants habitants d'une petite ville au pied des Alpes (Julie ou la Nouvelle Héloïse)* (Amsterdam, 1761).
6. Ibid.
7. Benedetta Craveri, *Madame Du Deffand et son monde*, French ed. (Paris, 1987).
8. Marie-Madeleine Martinet, *Art et nature en Grande-Bretagne au XVIIIe siècle* (Paris, 1980).
9. Craveri, *Madame Du Deffand et son monde*.
10. Rousseau, *La Nouvelle Héloïse*.
11. Stern, *A l'ombre de Sophie Arnould*.
12. "La Folie Monceau," in the catalogue of the exhibition *De Bagatelle à Monceau*.
13. Ibid.
14. Stern, *A l'ombre de Sophie Arnould*.
15. Charles-Joseph, Prince de Ligne, *Coup d'oeil sur Beloeil* (Beloeil, 1781).
16. Ibid.
17. Ibid.
18. Thomas Whately, *Observations on Modern Gardening* (London, 1770).
19. Jean-Marie Morel, *Théorie des jardins* (Paris, 1776).
20. Claude-Henri Watelet, *Essai sur les jardins* (1774).
21. Ibid.
22. Ibid.
23. Ibid.
24. Ibid.
25. Jean Starobinski, *L'invention de la liberté* (Geneva, 1964).
26. Ernest de Ganay, *Les jardins de France et leur décor* (Paris, 1949).
27. Nicolas Restif de la Bretonne, *Tableaux de la Vie ou Moeurs du XVIIIe siècle* (Paris, 1791).
28. Jean-François Marmontel, *Contes moraux* (Paris, 1779).
29. Watelet, *Essai sur les jardins*.
30. Charles-Joseph, Prince de Ligne, *Coup d'oeil sur Beloeil*.
31. Ernest de Ganay, "Plaisirs de Trianon," in *Jardin des Arts* (August 1959).
32. Watelet, *Essai sur les jardins*.
33. Ibid.
34. Ibid.
35. Abbé Jacques Delille, *Oeuvres (Les Jardins)* (Paris, 1786).
36. René-Louis Gerardin, marquis de Girardin, *De la composition des paysages* (Paris, 1777).
37. Ganay, *Les jardins de France*.
38. Monique Mosser, "Le château de Castille entre le néo-classicisme et le romantisme," in *Monuments Historiques*, no. 108 (1980).
39. Starobinski, *L'invention de la liberté*.

LIST OF ILLUSTRATIONS

PAINTINGS, DRAWINGS, ENGRAVINGS, AND MAPS

ILLUSTRATED AND ILLUMINATED BOOKS AND OTHER WORKS

SELECTED BIBLIOGRAPHY

Adams, William Howard. *The French Garden, 1500–1800*. New York, 1979.

André, E. *L'art des jardins: Traité général de la composition des parcs et jardins*. Paris, 1879.

Barton, S. *Monumental Follies: An Exposition on the Eccentric Edifices of Britain*. Worthing, Sussex, 1972.

Benoist-Méchin. *L'homme et ses jardins ou les métamorphoses du Paradis terrestre*. Paris, 1975.

Berrall, Julia S. *The Garden: An Illustrated History*. New York, 1966.

Blaikie, Thomas. *Diary of a Scotch Gardener at the French Court at the End of the Eighteenth Century*, introduction by Francis Birrell. London, 1931.

Bord, J. *Mazes and Labyrinths of the World*. London, 1976.

Borsi, Franco. *Ville e Giardini*. Novare, 1984.

Bouchart, F. X. *Jardins fantastiques*. Paris, 1982.

Chimay, J. de. *Les jardins à travers le monde*. Paris, 1962.

Clifford, Dereck. *A History of Garden Design*. London, 1962.

Coffin, David R., *The Villa d'Este at Tivoli*. Princeton, 1960.

Collins, George R., *Les bâtisseurs de rêve*. Paris, 1980.

Conner, P. *Oriental Architecture in the West*. London, 1979.

Cowell, F. R. *The Garden as a Fine Art: From Antiquity to Modern Times*. London, 1978.

————. *De Bagatelle à Monceau: Les Folies du XVIIIe siècle à Paris*. Catalogue of the exhibition at the Domaine de Bagatelle and the Musée Carnavalet. Paris, 1978–79.

Eckardt, G. *Verzeichnis der Bauten und Plastiken im Park von Sanssouci*. Potsdam, 1973.

Erdberg, E. von. *Chinese Influence on European Garden Structures*. Cambridge, Mass., 1936.

Eydoux, Henri-Paul. *Châteaux fantastiques*. Paris, 1969–73.

————. *Monuments curieux et sites étranges*. Paris, 1974.

Fox, Helen (Morgenthau). *André Le Nôtre, Garden Architect to Kings*. London, 1962.

Francastel, P. *La sculpture à Versailles: Essai sur les origines et l'évolution du goût français classique*. Paris, 1970.

Ganay, Ernest de. *Les jardins de France et leur décor*. Paris, 1949.

————. *Beaux jardins de France*. Paris, 1950.

————. *André Le Nôtre, 1613–1700*. Paris, 1962.

Godoli, A., and A. Natali. *Luoghi della Toscana medicea*. Florence, 1980.

Grimal, P. *L'art des jardins*. Paris, 1954.

Gromort, G. *Jardins d'Italie*. Paris, 1931.

————. *L'art des jardins*. Paris, 1934.

Guerniero, Giovanni Francesco. *Plans et desseins des bastiments, cascades et fontaines dont Charles, Landgrave de Hesse, Prince de Hersfeld, a décoré la montagne vulgairement nommée la Montagne de l'Hiver . . .* Rome, Cassel, 1749. (Original edition, 1706.)

Hager, L. *Nymphenburg, le château, le parc et les pavillons*, French edition. Paris, 1980.

Hansmann, W. *Gartenkunst der Renaissance und des Barock*. Cologne, 1983.

Harris, John. *The Palladians*. London, 1981.

Hautecoeur, L., *Les jardins, des dieux et des hommes*. Paris, 1959.

Hazlehurst, Franklin Hamilton. *Gardens of Illusion: The Genius of André Le Nôtre*. Nashville, 1980.

Hazlehurst, Franklin Hamilton, and Elisabeth B. Macdougall. *The French Formal Garden*. Washington, D.C., 1974.

Hirschfeld, C. C. L. *Anmerkungen über die Landhäuser und die Gartenkunst*. Leipzig, 1773.

————. *Theorie der Gartenkunst*. Leipzig, 1775.

————. *Theorie de l'Art des jardins*. Leipzig, 1779–85 (reprinted 1973).

Hunt, John D. *The Figure in the Landscape: Poetry, Painting and Gardening during the Eighteenth Century*. Baltimore, 1976.

Hussey, Christopher. *English Gardens and Landscapes, 1700–1750*. London, 1967.

Hyams, Edward S. *The English Garden*. London, 1964.

————. *A History of Gardens and Gardening*. London, 1971.

Jardins en France, 1760–1820: Pays d'illusion, terre d'expériences. Catalogue of the exhibition organized by the Caisse nationale des Monuments historiques, Paris, 1977.

Jones, B. *Follies and Grottoes*. London, 1974.

Kayser, B., and R. *L'amour des jardins célebré par les ecrivains*. Paris, 1986.

King, Ronald. *Quest for Paradise: A History of the World's Gardens*. New York, 1979.

Kraft, J. C. *Receuil d'Architecture civile . . . Jardins*, Paris, 1804.

──────. *Plans des plus beaux jardins pittoresques de France, d'Angleterre et d'Allemagne*. Paris, 1809.

Kretzulesco-Quaranta, Emanuela. *Les jardins du Songe: Poliphile et la mystique de la Renaissance*, French edition. Paris, 1976.

Laborde, Jean-Joseph de. *Description des nouveaux Jardins de la France*. Paris, 1808–16 (reprinted 1971).

Lassus, Baronne Simone de. "Les fabriques de Méréville à Jeurre," in *L'Information d'Histoire de l'Art*, no. 1 (1975).

Lazzaro-Bruno, C. "The Villa Lante at Bagnaia: An Allegory of Art and Nature," in *Art Bulletin 59* (1977).

Lemoine, P., and J. Girard. *Versailles aux couleurs du temps*. Paris, 1983.

Le Rouge, Georges-Louis. *Jardins Anglo-Chinois à la mode*. Paris, 1776–89.

Louis XIV, Manière de montrer les Jardins de Versailles, introduction by Simone Hoog. Paris, 1982.

Magnol-Malhache, V., and G. Weill. *Jardins et paysages des Hauts-de-Seine*. Catalogue of the exhibition at the Archives départementales des Hauts-de-Seine, Nanterre, 1982.

Magrini, G. *Grandi giardini d'Italia*. Milan, 1970.

Marie, A. *Jardins français classiques aux XVIIe et XVIIIe siècles*. Paris, 1949.

──────. *Jardins français crées à la Renaissance*. Paris, 1955.

──────. *Naissance de Versailles: Le château, les jardins*. Paris, 1968.

Martinet, Marie-Madeleine. *Art et nature en Grande-Bretagne au XVIIIe siècle: De l'harmonie classique au pittoresque du premier romantisme*. Paris, 1980.

Masson, Georgina. *Italian Gardens*. London, 1961.

Mauricheau-Beaupré, C. *Palais et jardins du Grand Siècle*. Paris, 1950.

Neubauer, E. *Lustgärten des Barock*. Salzburg, 1966.

Nobile, B. M. *I Giardini d'Italia*. Bologna, 1984.

Racine, M. *Architecture rustique des rocailleurs*. Paris, 1981.

Rohde, Eleanor S. *The Old English Gardening Books*. London, 1972.

Shepherd, John Chiene, and G. A. Jellicoe. *Italian Gardens of the Renaissance*. New York, 1966.

Siren, Osvald. *China and Gardens of Europe of the Eighteenth Century*. New York, 1950.

Soldini, F. M. *Il reale giardino di Boboli nella sua pianta e nelle su statue*. Florence, 1789 (reprinted 1976).

Thacker, Christopher. *The History of Gardens*. London, 1979.

Theurillat, Jacqueline. *Les mystères de Bomarzo et les jardins symboliques de la Renaissance*. Geneva, 1973.

Wiebenson, Dora. *The Picturesque Garden in France*. Princeton, 1978.

Willis, Peter. *Charles Bridgeman and the English Landscape Garden*. London, 1977.

Willis, Peter, and John D. Hunt, eds. *The Genius of the Place: The English Landscape Garden, 1620–1820*. London, 1975.

INDEX